The U.S.-Russian

Entente

That Saved the Union

By Konstantin George

Cover: adapted from original cover of *Campaigner* magazine Vol. 11, No. 5, July 1978 in which this study was first published

Amazon Print on Demand Edition

ISBN: 9781520974347

the Campaigner

CAMPAIGN FOR HUMANISM

The Campaigner is published by Campaigner Publications,Inc.and is the English Language journal of the National Caucus of Labor Committees. Current policies of the Labor Committees are stated in editorials; views expressed in signed articles are not necessarily those of either the Labor Committees or the editorial board.

Editorial Board
Nora Hamerman, Ken Kronberg
Nancy Spannaus, Carol White
Christopher White

Managing Editor
Paul Arnest

Production Editor
Diane Yue

Book Editor
Susan Parmacek Johnson

The Campaigner is published monthy 10 times per year except January and April by Campaigner Publications,Inc.,231 West 29th street,New York,New York 10001.
Subscriptions by mail are $19.00 for 10 issues in the U.S.A. and Canada.Air Mail subscriptions to other countries are $38.00 for 10 issues.
Application to mail at Second Class postage is pending at New York,N.Y.

ON THE COVER: The Union Army on parade in New York City, with the red, white and blue flags of the United States and Imperial Russia.   Cover design by Alan Yue.

Vol.11   No.5   July 1978

CONTENTS

Above: The original Contents page from the July 1978 edition of *Campaigner* magazine which contained this study.

THE U.S.-RUSSIAN ENTENTE THAT SAVED THE UNION

By Konstantin George

Note From the Editors

Americans tend to believe that our history is primarily local. In reality, the American Civil War was part of a global confrontation between the British Empire and forces pushing the "American System" model of scientific-industrial development for their own nations. This is thoroughly proven in this article. However, Konstantin George's hypothesis, that actions of Secretary of State Seward and Secretary of War Stanton were motivated by their secret allegiance to the British Empire, has since been disproven. With that caveat, what you are about to read is a treasure of American and world history.

The following is the complete text and graphics of the July 1978 edition of The Campaigner magazine feature article. --April, 2017

INTRODUCTION

The fact that the global axiom of British foreign policy has been the creation and maintenance of a United States-Soviet adversary relationship can be explained only with an examination of the shared humanist traditions of both modern superpowers. This study will document United States-Russia collaboration to win the American Civil War for the Union--the historical apex of a continuous political collaboration between the humanist elites of the two nations dating back to Benjamin Franklin.

A brief note here will serve to certify the impact on world history of that collaboration, even at its inception during the American Revolutionary War. It was a direct follower of Franklin, Epinus, a leader of the Russian Academy of Sciences, who drafted the famous League of Armed Neutrality Treaty--a Russian-led alliance that was key in creating the international strategic context in which the American Revolution succeeded.[1]

The crowning period of humanist U.S.-Russian collaboration was during the Lincoln Administration, when a wartime alliance between the United States and Russia was negotiated by U.S. ambassador to Russia Cassius Clay. America and Russia shared the conception of transforming this wartime pact into a permanent alliance based on the combination of developing Russia into a technologically progressive nation of 100 million and an industrialized U.S. with a population approaching 100 million by the end of the nineteenth century.

This combination the emerging national giants saw as an unbeatable axis for implementing worldwide technological progress--the "Grand Design," a world-ordering of sovereign nations committed to progress. Ambassador Clay, in fact, considered his own mission to be the forging of an alliance among the United States, Russia, and President Benito Juarez in Mexico, committed to the spread of republicanism around the globe.[2]

The Russian government of Czar Alexander II with which Lincoln and Clay negotiated the alliance was itself-- as were Lincoln and Clay--conscious followers of the great American political economist Henry Carey. From the czar on down, Russia's goals for economic growth were literally expounded as: "What you Americans call the 'American System,' we Russians must adopt as the 'Russian System.' "

Subsumed under the features of the Grand Design were the urgently necessary measures of the wartime alliance. During the Civil War itself, Russia's military weight and threats of reprisals against Britain and France prevented any British-led intervention against the Union.

Lincoln met heavy opposition in seeing through this policy. Then, as now, Britain used its U.S. agents-of-influence and press outlets to force the U.S. off the course to the Grand Design. The copperhead press and agents-of-influence like Secretary of State Seward in the cabinet repeatedly raised the "human rights" issue around the so-called "Polish right of secession" to argue against the entente with Russia. Lincoln was pilloried by the copperhead traitors for "cavorting with absolutism, Czarist oppression and brutality," etc., in the same way that

The October 1863 grand parade honoring the Russian fleet in New York harbor, shown passing Trinity Church on its way up Broadway. From Harper's Weekly, October 17, 1863.

London's modern propaganda mills have inundated this nation with the bogeys of "totalitarianism" and "communism."

Lincoln, unlike his professed followers of today, never caved in to such nonsense. The implementation of the Grand Design, and its necessary precondition of winning the Civil War, were his Administration's paramount policy goals. So-called policies being advocated that acted to subvert or compromise the U.S.-Russian entente as the cornerstone of Lincoln's foreign policy were summarily dismissed. Lincoln and Clay knew very well where our nation's enemy resided--in London.

THE U.S.-RUSSIAN ENTENTE

The two greatest victories against Guelph monetarism in modern history were the American Revolution and the preservation of the American Union in the U.S. Civil War. The Civil War was no less global in implication and character than the American Revolution. The American Civil War was a global political war that came--several times--within a hair's breadth of global shooting war. The global battle lines were drawn between two international alliances: the Union and the Russian Empire, arrayed against the Confederacy in alliance with England and France--the Russell-Palmerston alliance with their tool, "Petit" Louis Napoleon (III).

The Union's survival and ultimate victory was strategically anchored by an unshakeable alliance with the Russian Empire during the entire Civil War. The existence of that alliance was the sole reason that the Union was able to wage the war without facing combined English and French military intervention, which would in all likelihood have meant the successful balkanization of these United States. That nothing of the sort transpired, as we shall see, was due solely to the influential "American" faction in Russia, to whose outlook Alexander II tended. This faction stuck to its guns, despite all British threats, to ensure the survival and development of the United States for the common interest of Russia and America.

At several of the most critical junctures of the Civil War the Lord Russell-Petit Napoleon axis was on the verge of declaring war on the Union. Each time they were forced to weigh the consequences of a fully mobilized Russia's declaration of war on England and France. Russia's huge land armies were ready to roll over the Ottoman Empire and India, thus ending British political domination of an area extending in a great arc from the Balkans through the Middle East to London's subcontinental "jewel" of India. Such a response by Russia, horrifying enough to the Lords of the British Empire, was clearly but the first in a series of disastrous consequences for Britain should London have decided to move against the forces of Lincoln in the United States.

A British-French declaration of war on the Union, entailing war with the Russian Empire as well, represented the crossing of a tripwire that would have produced a nonlinear effect on the political geometry of Europe which would have proved disastrous to Britain. A global shooting war between world alliances led by Britain and the U.S. and Russia respectively would have forced the reality principle to assert itself in Germany, destroying once and for all the carefully orchestrated British "steering" of German policy and possibly turning Germany against Britain, much the same way as Germany went "the wrong way" during World War I. This can be summarized as follows.

Had Russia not lined up with the Union, a wavering London-dominated Bisrnarckian Germany, with no anti-British Continental powers nearby, would have been able to swing nationalist elements in the German leadership into joining Britain and France as a junior partner. The fact that Russia allied with the Union and mobilized to fight if necessary, did more than "keep Bismarck honest." It guaranteed that if a global shooting war erupted, German national interests, which could not tolerate the elimination of the United States and Russia and a Europe under the complete domination of England and Petit Napoleon, would lawfully assert their control over German policy and move against London. In short, the "concert of powers" rigged game that had characterized European affairs since the Congress of Vienna would be over.

The means of British political control over the continent would have gone up like an exploding cigar in the faces of Russell and Palmerston. These then were the consequences that the Empire elites had to face each time they were tempted to intervene militarily against Lincoln and impose a "final solution" to the American problem. Each time, cursing bitterly at "the Russians," they pulled back from the brink.

The cornerstone of Britain's operational policy, from no later than 1860 on, was to dismember both the United States and Russia. This "removal of obstacles" was the prelude to enacting a Rothschildian monetarist "new world order," devoid of sovereign nation states, an order centered on a British-controlled Grand Confederacy, labeled by British policymakers "The United States of Europe."

On the United States side, the British fostering of and support of the Confederacy, and their well-known plans, pending successful outcome of the secession, to further fragment and subdivide the Union, need no elaboration. A simultaneous policy of dismantling the Russian Empire along "nationality" lines was fully operational. Its full-scale application was merely awaiting the necessary precondition of a balkanized Union here. Then, all secessionist hell would break loose in Russia. The direct opening gambit of this drive was the launching of the British-inspired and conducted Polish uprising, six weeks after the Confederate attack on Fort Sumter, in June 1861.

Fort Sumter and a U.S. Civil War in April 1861, a Polish uprising against Russia in June 1861. These were the immediate events which set into motion the creation of the U.S.-Russian entente, conceived of by both countries as the international strategic vehicle to destroy the British Empire. The story of the conscious creation of this alliance by American and Russian "Whigs" now deserves to be documented. Americans can gape in astonishment at what "the books" have hidden from them.

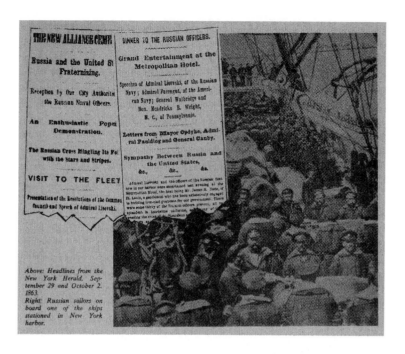

Above: Headlines from the New York Herald, September 29 and October 2, 1863.
Right: Russian sailors on board one of the ships stationed in New York harbor.

THE ENTENTE'S TRADITION

We have asserted that the Civil War alliance marked the apex pf a longstanding collaboration between the humanist political-scientific-military elites of the United States and Russia. The Lincoln administration did not stumble upon the notion of a U.S.-Russian alliance as the strategic key to the Grand Design's implementation. Conversely, the Russian government headed by Prince Alexander Gorchakov under the reign of Alexander II, was not "seized" by some sudden burst of inspiration, or crafty opportunism, in the spring of 1861. What was achieved during the Civil War by the two "superpowers" was the consummation of a quarter-century-long bitter struggle by United States and Russian Neoplatonists against the London-orchestrated political machines in their respective nations. From 1844 to 1860, British agents of influence repeatedly sabotaged earlier potentialities for the alliance to develop. It was a quarter century punctured with missed opportunities and tough lessons learned, as a result of which the strategic perceptions and capacities for action of the foremost of the United States' Whigs and their Russian counterparts were shaped and increasingly perfected.

The bedrock foundation of United States-Russian collaboration, the product of the political influence exerted within Russia by the networks organized by Benjamin Franklin in the Russian Academy of Science (whose leading members such as Epinus, were themselves conscious followers of the tradition of technological progress established by the collaboration of Leibniz and Peter the Great) and through the American Philosophical Society, was established in the 1763-1815 period. The impact of the American Founding Fathers on the Russia of that period was phenomenal. Wedded to the already established Petrovian traditions of transforming Russia into an industrial giant was an added dimension in which the Epinus-Count Panin "American" elite defined Russia's progressive historical mission. National purpose, for Russia from 1776 on, defined Russia's foreign policy as the creation of the global political conditions in which the young American Republic could fulfill its industrial capitalist transformation without overt interference from London beyond tolerable bounds.

In the period from 1776 to 1815, Russia twice played a crucial role in safeguarding the existence of America. During the Revolutionary War, the acceptance of Epinus' draft of a Treaty of Armed Neutrality by Premier Count

Panin was not only key in ending Britain's plans for building an anti-American coalition in Europe, but also marked a signal triumph by the Russian Franklinites in wresting political hegemony away from the perverse Benthamite, Prince Potemkin. In the War of 1812, our "Second War of Independence," Russia, under Alexander I, submitted a near-ultimatum to England to hastily conclude an honorable peace with the United States and abandon all English claims of territorial aggrandizement. The American negotiators themselves were the first to confirm that only the application of Russian pressure produced the sudden *volte-face* in Britain's attitude that achieved the Treaty of Ghent. The physical reality that Russian troops, as a result of the concluding campaigns of the Napoleonic Wars, occupied a swath of European territory from Berlin to Paris, caused the pragmatic Guelphs to elect not to antagonize the "Russian Giant." One may also note that directly prior to the War of 1812, through the negotiating efforts of John Quincy Adams (at the time United States Minister to Russia), exponential growth rates in U.S.-Russian trade were achieved. By 1811, the United States had by far and away become Russia's largest trading partner. [3] All these events, and others too numerous to recount, were well-remembered in the United States and Russia of the 1840s to 1860s period. [4]

The resurgence of the American Whig movement in the 1840s was the prime catalyst in breaking the deepening demoralization that had sapped Russia's patriots in the post-Treaty of Vienna era. Witnessing America free itself of the abominations of the Jackson-Van Buren years, a Russian faction headed by Prince Stroganov and Miliutin (later to become War Minister in 1862) launched a fight to win over Nicholas I to a policy of beginning Russia's industrialization, abolishing serfdom, and allying with the United States. A significant though short-lived shift in Russian policy occurred. Nicholas initiated a development program by commissioning an American team headed by Major Whistler to supervise construction of Russia's first full-length railroad from St. Petersburg to Moscow.[5]

At this stage, Russia was evolving rapidly towards proposing an alliance with the United States, and, internally, was on the verge of adopting wide-ranging reforms, starting with the abolition of serfdom, drafted by Stroganov and Miliutin. The key governing success or failure of this policy evolution lay in the American policy to Russia. The decisive conjuncture occurred under the fight Americans know as the "Oregon Question" and the slogan, "Fifty-four-forty or fight"--America's crisis with England over the Northwest Territories. In March 1845, Nicholas I conveyed to President Polk via Robert J. Walker that Russia was willing to cede Alaska to the United States, provided the United States maintained its claim to the Pacific Coast up to the line of fifty-four degrees, forty minutes north latitude--which marked the southern boundary of Russian America.[6] Russia was saying very simply: "If you Americans seize all of England's North American Pacific coastline, we will give you our territory as well, and back you in any resulting crisis with England." Out of stupidity, or worse, Polk rebuffed Nicholas, "amicably" sold out to England with the forty-ninth parallel "compromise," and turned south to wage war on Mexico, using this as a convenient *fait accompli* to present to the outraged Whigs ("We can't fight two wars at one time") to justify the sell-out.

The negative repercussions in Russia were massive. The British faction in the Russian nobility played up Polk's sell-out, which left Russia alone to face London's rage, to the hilt. The nearly actualized reforms (which the zero-growth baboon-like provincial nobility hated) were quashed, railroad building and industrial progress stagnated.

The event that completed the molding and toughening of the commitment to entente of the Russian and American humanists was the 1853-56 Crimean War. Russia's humiliation, and the acute realization that British policy was orienting toward actual dismemberment of the Russian Empire, together with the accrued lessons of the missed opportunities of the 1844-46 period, burned in the requisite lessons. The fundamental point that could no longer be ignored was that Russia would have no security as a nation, let alone prosperity, unless it urgently committed itself to abolishing serfdom and industrializing to fortify itself against the British Monarchy. The significance of the Crimean War was recognized with equal emphasis by American Whigs.

To most Americans today, the image of the Crimean War connotes a war waged by "civilized" England and France against "semi-barbarous" Russia, with the clearest image being the romantic drivel of Tennyson's "Charge of the Light Brigade." In 1854, most of the American population was avowedly pro-Russian in its attitude toward that conflict. The Whig press, led by the *New York Herald*, was openly advocating a United States-Russian alliance, in response to Russia's repeated requests for assistance.[7]

This was no hysteria campaign. The United States Minister to St. Petersburg, T.H. Seymour, in a line of argument that is paradigmatic of the Whig thinking at the time, repeatedly warned the fool President Pierce and his anglophile Secretary of State William Marcy, what Britain was up to. The letter to Marcy dated April 13, 1854 is exemplary:

> ". . . the danger is that the Western powers of Europe, who, after they have humbled the Czar, will domineer the rest of Europe, and thus have the leisure to turn their attention to American affairs."[8]

Under the rotten Pierce and Buchanan administrations, alliance was out of the question, but the process that was to define the projected contents of the Grand Design was developed in the years 1855 to 1861.

THE STRATEGIC SITUATION ON THE EVE OF CIVIL WAR

From 1855 to 1861, the Russian "American faction" led by the new Czar, Alexander II, Foreign Minister Gorchakov, and an in-depth, American-spawned, top-level cadre in the Russian Naval Ministry under the Grand Duke Constantine (which included the Civil War period's Ministers of War, Miliutin, and Finance, Reutern, to name but a few of the notables who were schooled in the Naval Ministry), waged unconditional war within Russia to uproot the evil Boyars, the feudal provincial nobility who formed the social backbone of the British Lobby within Russia.   Simultaneously, Gorchakov et al. repeatedly put forward to the United States as the key elements of global development policies, the components of the Grand Design. Gorchakov, the central figure in determining the American faction's policy moves, was not overly concerned, per se, during this period, that the United States government, under the wretch Buchanan, would ignore and reject these Russian offers.   His goal was much more sophisticated, to gain the acceptance of the American Whig *counterpole* of the entente foreign policy perspective. This goal was achieved.

Thus, from 1855 on, Russia renewed as a standing offer the donation of Alaska to the United States, under the anti-British Empire conditions enunciated first in 1845. This standing offer was followed up with numerous substantial project offers to American capitalists, which from the present world historical vantage point, are strikingly similar to the May 1978 Brezhnev-Schmidt Summit proposals and deals. The correspondence of the U.S.

Czar Alexander II: "I shall accept the recognition of the independence of the Confederate States by France and Great Britain as a casus belli."

THE U.S.-RUSSIAN ENTENTE   17

Minister to St. Petersburg from 1857 to 1860, Pickens, provides irrefutable proof of the Russian policy and organizing approach. Most notable in this regard were the Russian government's Siberian-Far East and Near East development packages. In 1858, Russia proposed an agreement with the United States for joint cooperation in developing trade with China. In conjunction with this offer, Russia unilaterally opened the entire Amur River basin region (the Maritime Provinces of Siberia) to free trade with the United States.[9] The series of development proposals had begun as early as June 18, 1855, when Russia offered to extend its facilities to the United States in negotiating a commercial treaty with Persia, a step that would have begun the process of ending British hegemony in the region.[10] During the 1858-1860 period, United States ambassador to Russia Pickens wrote on numerous occasions urging United States-Russian joint trade and economic expansion to effect a strategic shift against England.

On January 12, 1859, Pickens wrote: "Russia can hold a more certain control over Europe by her influence in the East, and she wishes the U.S. to tap the China trade from the East in order to keep England out."[11]

Pickens, May 26, 1859: "Russia could be the arbiter of Europe, and . . . the U.S. without danger from France and England would be left free to settle American [meaning Hemispheric] interests, and might by trade become one of the arbiters of the power of the world."[12]

On April 17, 1860, after talks with officials of the Russian Foreign Ministry, Pickens conveyed an urgent warning to Washington that a full United States-British rupture was close, concluding with this policy advice: ". . . it is thus imperative that we keep an able Minister here [for the incoming new United States Administration in 1861] . . . to produce through Russia a strong organization of the Baltic States against the power of England."[13]

The contents of this letter is of extraordinary historical significance, as it testifies directly that the humanist networks of the United States and Russia were convinced correctly--that danger of a British-inspired conflict against the United States was rapidly increasing. Pickens' advice for United States policy to undertake the creation of a Russian-led European alliance against England expressed precisely both the intent and content of Benjamin Franklin's creation through the Petrovian Neoplatonic elite in the Russia of Catherine the Great of the League of Armed Neutrality. Pickens' policy, reflecting the view of Alexander II and Gorchakov--as in the case of the Franklin-spawned League--was a policy geared to imminent or actual war conditions, conditions of acute danger to the survival of the American Republic. As we shall document, the Russian government had arrived at precisely such an evaluation in the spring of 1860, and under Gorchakov's direct personal supervision dispatched a top-level covert intelligence mission to the United States, a team that, with no exaggeration, played a decisive role in stymying the Confederacy's 1861 "blitzkrieg" strategy.

With the advent of the Lincoln administration, the United States-British rupture came to a head. The building global strategic shift against the British Guelph obscenity dictated London's response. All the Russian

President Lincoln: "Please assure His Majesty that the whole nation appreciates this new manifestation of friendship."

economic development proposals of the proceeding five years were ripe for implementation. United States Whigs, led by Lincoln, Clay, Admiral Farragut, and others, were preparing to launch a policy to develop Russia industrially and militarily.

In the Western Hemisphere, the end of British control over Latin America and Canada was considered imminent. Prodevelopment Latin American government officials understood very clearly the positive implications for their region of a successful outcome of the fight waged by the United States-Russian alliance against the British Empire. The deputy Foreign Minister of Colombia emotionally expressed this sentiment: "The United States Civil War is a step in the direction of the United States' mission, to regenerate the whole continent, and .   . . the United States and Russia, the two great Northern powers, 'Colossi of two continents,' if they could identify their interests, would be the surest bulwark of the independence of the world." [14]

Canada was all but ready to be annexed by the United States in 1861 (with hardly a shot needed to be, fired) had the Confederacy operation not been launched by Great Britain. Under London's cultural relativist policies governing their colonies, the Canadian West (i.e., at that time all territory west of Ontario), in contrast to the aggressive economic development policies pursued south of the forty-ninth parallel, was relegated to remain forever the habitat of the beaver, the caribou, a handful of British colonial administrators, and other of the lower species. In the middle and late 1850s, large numbers of adventurous Americans settled in this huge western region (the present provinces of Manitoba, Saskatchewan, Alberta and British Columbia), founding towns and schools, and running their own regional governments.[15]

By 1860, the United States government was receiving a tidal wave of petitions from Western Canada urging annexation to the United States. Similar agitation was widespread in Lower Canada (Quebec). We will let the *Nor Wester*, the newspaper in the Red River settlement that serviced the Western region, eloquently spell out "why" such annexation was being demanded. The editorial, a ringing indictment of the British System, was written by educated townspeople, very much in the vein of the language of Americans in the early 1770s: "England's policies leave us no choice but to break."

From the *Nor Wester*, in the year 1860:

"The peculiar system of government which prevails in this country bids fair to drive us into annexation to the United States. What is the use of being connected with Britain when the connection is merely nominal? It is a mere name, an empty sound, a meaningless design . . . . For years the home government has looked on us with indifference. It is surely no matter of surprise that public sentiment is in favor of annexation to the United States. The Red River country is the center of a most valuable British appendage. Is it the interest or duty of the imperial authorities to alienate the sympathies and chill the loyalty

Foreign Minister Gorchakov: "We desire above all things the maintenance of the American Union as one indivisible nation."

Ambassador Cassius Clay: "I did more than any man to overthrow slavery. I carried Russia with us."

of the people here by such careless neglect? We are indebted to Americans for the only route that there is to and from this country . . . . Commercial activity has been infused into our system. Home industry is stimulated, and all this brought about by Americans. In fact, why so anxious to be connected with Britain when such connection is nominal and fruitless. Let us rather seek to form part and parcel of the great country from which we are receiving and will ever receive such practical benefits." [16]

Imminent prospects of Canada's annexation to the United States were prominently recognized in the United States Whig press, while the Minnesota State legislature sent to Congress the first State memorialization setting forth the commercial and political advantages that would be gained from the Americanization of the Canadian West.[17]

This then represents the actual strategic conjuncture and prospects in 1860, when Britain utilized the last portion of the traitor Buchanan's term in office to launch the Southern Secession.

Sensation in the Happy Family caused by the Reception of the Russians at New York.

From Harper's Weekly, October 1863.

ABRAHAM LINCOLN'S FOREIGN POLICY

President Lincoln's top-priority foreign policy following Fort Sumter was forging a strategic alliance with Russia. Lincoln was aware that under the political hegemony of Foreign Minister Gorchakov, Russia was modernizing. The freeing of the serfs had occurred in the spring of 1861, and a vast program of railroad building was underway. Lincoln was also aware that both Gorchakov and the Czar were pro-American and unswervingly anti-British. The latter point did not represent "inside" knowledge only. Even Marx, for example, wrote unequivocally that Alexander II "has no liking for the English."

By no later than May, 1861, Lincoln was acting on his policy that a U.S.-Russian alliance to counter Britain was highest priority. In choosing his personal envoy to St. Petersburg, Lincoln went outside all normal channels, and selected the nephew of American Whig statesman Henry Clay, Cassius Marcellus Clay; as his ambassador to Russia.

Clay's mission to Russia was twofold. As an integral part of his role in negotiating a strategic alliance, Clay consciously viewed his primary task as developing and consolidating the existing Russian elite into an unbeatable political machine, such that it would acquire the talent and muscle necessary to ruthlessly see through Russia's full-scale industrialization. Clay brought with him many copies of Henry Carey's book on political economy, hand delivering them to Alexander II, Gorchakov, Prince

Dolgoruky, the Navy Minister, the Grand Duke Constantine, and a host of other high officials and industrialists too numerous to_mention. Clay toured the major cities, delivering speeches to thunderous applause from captains of industry, regional and national government officials, and merchants, expounding on the need for Russia to rapidly industrialize. Clay's speeches on industrialization and Carey's policies were reprinted throughout the Russian press. Henry Carey literally became a household word in Russia.

From Clay's *Memoirs*, we quote here his own account of the effect of his industrialization drive in Russia:

> A large class of manufacturers was aggregated about Moscow . . . . England was our worst enemy in the world and I sought out how I might most injure her. Russia with her immense lands and resources, and great population, was a fine field for British manufactures, and she had made the most of it. I procured the works of H.C. Carey of Philadelphia, and presented them to the Foreign Office, to the Emperor himself. So, it began to be understood that I was the friend of home industry--the "Russian System." I encouraged the introduction of American arms, sewing machines, and all that, as far as I could; the mining of petroleum, and its manufacture; and got the United States to form a treaty preventing the violation of trademarks in the commerce of the two nations. So, when I was invited to Moscow, it was intimated that a tariff speech would be quite acceptable. A dinner was given me by the corporate powers of Moscow.

. . . They got up a magnificent dinner; and with the American and Russian flags over my head, I made a regular tariff speech. It was translated into Russian as I spoke, and received immense applause. It was also put in Russian newspapers and into pamphlet form, circulated in the thousands all over the Empire. This touched England in the tenderest spot; and whilst Sir A. Buchanan and lady (the British ambassador, who was present) was too well bred to speak of it, one of the attaches was less discreet and shouted how much I threatened British trade. The dinner was photographed at the time.

I found that the argument which I had made for years in the South, in favor of free labor and manufactures, as co-factors, was well understood in Russia; and since emancipation and education have taken a new projectile force, railroads and manufactures have the same propulsion as is now exhibited in the "Solid South" [the last segment refers to Clay's lifelong efforts to industrialize the South].[18]

Clay's Moscow tariff speech concluded with the Russian industrialists present toasting the "Great American Economist, Henry Carey." The epistemological quality of the Moscow speech can be readily gathered from the ' following extract:

. . . The true policy is not to declare absolutely for free trade or protection, but to subject both systems to a wise statesmanship. As a general rule, every nation should manufacture its own raw products into the highest form of value, and then export them to foreign countries; this is the trade which being most useful to each, would best promote the common interests of all nations."[19]

With equal vigor, Clay went to work paving the way for the military alliance that would dismantle the British Empire, and in conjunction with this negotiated with Russia the opening of the Far Eastern development side of the Grand Design, the construction of a Washington-St. Petersburg cable via the Pacific through San Francisco and Vladivostok. The military alliance perspective and the strategic importance of the Trans-Pacific cable were clearly formulated in a letter from Clay to Seward dated August 3, 1861:

> We shall probably in union with Russia land an army at no distant day to settle accounts with England in China and the Indies [India]. We must never let her pass the Isthmus. The time has come for us to assume the lead in all the liberal governments of the West.

Clay went on to defend the treaty for the United States-Russian cable link:

> If we have to battle England on the sea, and should Russia be our ally, we shall have means of much earlier intelligence than she . . . . I think ourselves fortunate in having this great power as our sincere friend. We should keep up this friendly feeling, which will finally give us an immense market for our commerce, and give us a most powerful ally in common danger. We will and must take a common interest in the affairs of Europe.[20]

After the war, Clay summarized his mission as follows:

I did more than any man to overthrow slavery. I carried Russia with us and thus prevented what would have been a strong alliance of France, England, and Spain against us, and thus saved the nation.[21]

Contrary to the scribbled accounts of the wretched Fabian historians, this was no postwar afterthought. The entente concept of Clay and Lincoln was developed in full, in writing, in a Clay dispatch to Lincoln from St. Petersburg, dated July 25, 1861.

I saw at a glance where the feeling of England was. They hoped for our ruin. They are jealous of our power. They care neither for the North nor the South. They hate both. The London *Times* . . . in concluding its comments on your message [Lincoln's July 5, 1861 message to Congress] says: "And when we prefer a frank recognition of Southern independence by the North to the policy avowed in the President's message, it is solely because we foresee as bystanders that this is the issue in which after infinite loss and humiliation the contest must result." And that is the tone of England everywhere . . . if England would not favor us whilst following the lead of the antislavery policy--she will never be our friend. She will now if disaster comes upon our arms, join our enemies. Be on your guard.[22]

England the adversary can "never be our friend," reported Clay. What was to be done? Continuing with Clay's communication to Lincoln, there is no ambiguity in answering that question:

All the Russian journals are for us. In Russia we have a friend. The time is coming when she will be a powerful one for us. The emancipation [of the serfs] move is the beginning of a new era and new strength. She has immense lands, fertile and undeveloped in the Amoor country, with iron and other minerals. Here is where she must make the centre of her power against England. Joined with our Navy on the Pacific coast we will one day drive her [England] from the Indies: The source of her power: and losing which she will fall.[23]

An earlier communication to Lincoln elaborated United States contingencies should England declare war:

In case of war with England, Canada should be seized, money sent into Ireland and India to stir up revolt, slaves as property should be summarily confiscated; while extending the olive branch in case the rebels lay down their arms and return to duty and the Union.[24]

The July 25 communication concluded with advice to Lincoln to "extend the blockade to every. possible point of entry, so that if England does intervene--she will be the aggressor before all the world. Don't trust her in anything."[25]

In this earliest phase of the developing entente, the Russians were pro-American, though cautious. The caution was a lawful expression of a legitimate Russian concern. The Russians demanded to know if Lincoln would stand firm and fight the conflict through to preserve the Union. This was precisely the line of questioning of the Czar's first meeting with Clay in early July 1861, culminating with the question of what [the] Union would do should England intervene. Clay advised Lincoln: "I told the Emperor we did not care what England did, that her interference would tend to unite us the more."[26]

After this U.S. reassurance, Russia stood firmly behind its U.S. alliance. The entente policy was elaborated in a lengthy personal communication from Russian Foreign Minister Gorchakov to President Lincoln, dated July 10, 1861:

> From the beginning of the conflict which divides the United States of America, you have been desired to make known to the federal government the deep interest with which our August Master [Czar Alexander II] has been observing the development of a crisis which puts in question the prosperity and even the existence of the Union.
>
> The Emperor profoundly regrets that the hope of a peaceful solution is not realized and that American citizens, already in arms against each other, are ready to let loose upon their country the most formidable of the scourges of political society--civil war.
>
> For the more than eighty years that it has existed the American Union owes its independence, its towering rise, and its progress, to the concord of its members, consecrated, under the auspices of its illustrious founders, by institutions which have been able to reconcile union with liberty. This union has been fruitful. It has exhibited to the world the

spectacle of a prosperity without example in
the annals of history.

It would be deplorable if, after so conclusive
an experience, the United States should be
hurried into a breach of the solemn compact
which up to this time has made their power.

In spite of the diversity of their constitutions
and of their interests, and perhaps even because
of this diversity, Providence seems to urge
them to draw closer the traditional bond which
is the basis and the very condition of their
political existence. In any event, the sacrifices
which they might impose upon themselves to
maintain it are beyond comparison with those
which dissolution would bring after it. United,
they perfect themselves; isolated, they are
paralyzed.[27]

What we have quoted from this most extraordinary
historical document delineating Russian foreign policy
toward the United States destroys the British
historiographical myth that the Russian-American alliance
was a historical "aberration" in which both powers came
together on an "I can use the other guy" basis, and in which
"all the Russians cared about was the balance of power."
The concluding portion of this document, written by
Gorchakov and read and approved by Alexander II, puts
the final nail in the coffin of monetarist historiography on
this question:[28]

The struggle which unhappily has just arisen
can neither be indefinitely prolonged, nor lead
to the total destruction of one of the parties.
Sooner or later it will be necessary to come to

some settlement, which may enable the divergent interests now actually in conflict to coexist.

The American nation would then give proof of high political wisdom in seeking in common such a settlement before a useless effusion of blood, a barren squandering of strength and of public riches, and acts of violence and reciprocal reprisals shall have come to deepen an abyss between the two parties, to end in their mutual exhaustion, and in the ruin, perhaps irreparable of their commercial and political power.

Our August Master cannot resign himself to such deplorable anticipations . . . as a sovereign animated by the most friendly sentiments toward the American Union. *This union is not simply in our eyes an element essential to the universal political equilibrium. It constitutes, besides, a nation to which our August Master and all Russia have pledged the most friendly interest; for the two countries, placed at the two extremities of the world, both in the ascending period of their development appear called to a natural community of interests and of sympathies, of which they have given mutual proofs to each other* [emphasis added].

The preceding considerations . . . attest the lively solicitude of the Emperor, in presence of the dangers which menace the American Union, and the sincere wishes His Majesty entertains for the maintenance of that great work, so laboriously raised, which appeared so rich in future.

The officers of the Russian fleet in New York shown in dress uniform, engraved from a photograph which appeared in Harper's Weekly, November 7, 1863. From left: Captain Zelenoi, Captain Boutakov, Captain Federovski, Admiral Lessovsky, Captain Kopitov, Captain Kraemer, Captain Lundh.

. . . In every event the American nation
may count on the most cordial sympathy on the
part of our August Master during the serious
crisis which it is passing through at present.[29]

Lincoln was deeply moved on receipt of this Russian
policy statement, telling the Russian ambassador: "Please
inform the Emperor of our gratitude and assure His
Majesty that the whole nation appreciates this new
manifestation of friendship. Of all the communications we
have received from the European governments, this is the
most loyal." Lincoln then requested permission, which
was granted, to give the widest possible publicity to the
Russian message.[30]

This last point is crucial. The United States-Russian
alliance was no secret pact. Quite the contrary. By mutual
agreement between the two nations, the arrangement was
given as much publicity as possible, as were the reasons
behind it and its absolute necessity to the Union. Only
later was the historic entente sold by anglophile historians
as a Russian move for balance on the European continent.

RUSSIAN INTELLIGENCE AIDS THE UNION

As we intimated earlier, Russia's covert assistance
capability on behalf of the cause of the Union was in place
the moment the Civil War began. Acting on the basic
policy evaluation undertaken in the spring of 1860 that a
United States-British rupture was imminent, Gorchakov
dispatched a trusted officer in the Russian intelligence
service, Colonel Charles DeArnaud, to the United States in

June 1860. DeArnaud, with no exaggeration, was a hero of
the first rank, and by no means a mere "spy." In an 1890
book describing his mission DeArnaud wrote:

> I arrived in the United States for the second
> time in June, 1860 . . . . Being a Russian,
> knowing the friendly sentiments of the Russian
> government towards the United States as an
> entirety and hearing daily the threats of
> secession and war in the event of Lincoln's
> election, I took particular pains to ascertain
> whether all this talk was merely the froth on the
> surface, or . . .
>
> I was so engaged up to April 1861, when
> Fort Sumter roused the sleeping lion of loyalty
> in the North . . . . To me the whole question
> had assumed a very serious aspect. While
> travelling in the South I saw that extensive
> preparations were being made, not merely for
> local operations, but for general campaigns,
> and frequently heard from Southern gentlemen
> that it was the intention of the Confederate
> leaders to march and capture Washington and
> declare terms of peace north of the Potomac.[31]

DeArnaud, after evaluating all his intelligence, decided
that the move on Washington was a feint, and that the real
Confederate strategy was to stage an aura-of-power
"blitzkrieg" into the North proper in the Western theater of
operations, taking advantage of the Confederacy's short-
run military preponderance over the still-to-be-mobilized
Union Army in the initial period of the war.

DeArnaud was sent, under Russian Foreign Ministry
orders, west to Governor Lovell H. Rousseau of Kentucky
(Clay's home state), whom he briefed. Rousseau in turn

promptly dispatched the Russian colonel to his friend, General Fremont, then organizing the Union Army of the West, to serve as a personal assistant to the General.[32]

The details of DeArnaud's exploits would require a book in themselves. From August 3, 1861, when Fremont appointed him as a special aide on his staff in effective charge of all Union Army intelligence for the Western theater of operations,[33] DeArnaud was repeatedly and personally credited with drafting, plans--based on his unerringly accurate intelligence--that consistently deployed the numerically disadvantaged Union forces to "the right place every time," preempting every Confederate attempt to launch their offensive into the North--the offensive that was to give the appearance of Confederate victory that England was depending on to justify its intended early recognition of the Confederate states and accompanying move to preempt the Union blockade of the secessionist states.

In summary, DeArnaud's achievements were first to warn Fremont of the Confederacy's first offensive plans, which determined the Union to undertake a much more rapid mobilization in Indiana, Illinois and Missouri than would otherwise have occurred.[34]   Second, DeArnaud masterminded and executed successful deception and disinformation operations that repeatedly caused the Confederate commanders to move far more cautiously than objective considerations warranted. And, third, he played a decisive role in motivating the Union decision to build a large number of ironclad gunboats for the River fleet, whose rapid construction gave the Union complete naval superiority in the West, and, more importantly, a "no risk" capability to launch raids against virtually all Confederate strongpoints, depots, etc., along the key rivers of the region. This forced the Confederates to draw off a much higher proportion of their Western troops for garrison duty.[35]

Colonel DeArnaud preempted another Confederate offensive in September, 1861, when his intelligence blew the whistle on General Polk's attempt to take Paducah. Grant beat Polk to the city by six hours. The Russian colonel described his coup, following an extended stay behind enemy lines, as follows:

> A delay of six hours would have resulted in the triumphant execution of Polk's campaign, the enemy would have commanded the Ohio, Tennessee, Cumberland, and Mississippi rivers, would have crossed into Southern Illinois, captured St. Louis, and transferred the war to the Union States, confirming the wavering sentiments of thousands in those States to the Southern side, and procured from European powers the recognition of the Confederacy, and the consequent triumph of the Secession movement. Such vast results therefore hinged upon the occupation and retention of Paducah, the commanding strategic point of the campaign.[36]

DeArnaud repeatedly went on missions behind enemy lines, each time returning with information that enabled Union commanders to preempt enemy offensives. He, together with Fremont, was responsible for the drafting of the Union Army's offensive plans that were subsequently implemented in the Grant campaign of 1862.[37]

In February 1862, DeArnaud was recalled to Russia, where he arrived at the end of the month. He was immediately summoned to give a series of detailed intelligence briefings to Gorchakov. United States ambassador Clay was present at some of these sessions.[38]

We shall let DeArnaud himself tell the remainder of his story:

> On reaching the Russian capital, I was summoned to repair to the Foreign Office, at the request of the great Premier of the Russian Empire, Prince Gorchakov, as he had been told that I understood and correctly appreciated the relative positions of the contending forces in America, and consequently was likely to give him serviceable information about the struggle and its probable result. In this interview I enumerated the various successes obtained by General Fremont, and assured him that the effect upon the Confederates of the Union occupation of the Tennessee and the Cumberland rivers, and of the strategic positions held by the Union forces was so disastrous to their fortunes that they had been compelled to abandon offensive moves and to place themselves wholly on the defensive. I told him that I thought that the crushing of the Confederacy by the Union forces was only a matter of time . . . so long as the blockade was effectually maintained, and France and England did not interfere to raise it, as had been threatened, the South was at an enormous and constantly increasing disadvantage.
>
> Prince Gorchakov then inquired whether the United States had vessels and other naval

forces sufficient to maintain the efficiency of the blockade.

As DeArnaud did not have precise estimates on this question, Gorchakov replied:

> I shall find out whether they have vessels enough to maintain the blockade, and if they haven't, we have! [Exclamation in original.] The Emperor, my August Master will not permit anyone to interfere with this blockade, even if he has to risk another allied war! [Exclamation original.] [39]

Russia's commitment to the alliance was solid. Faced with this commitment, England worked assiduously, through her dupes and agents of influence in the United States to contain the global impact and potential of the entente.

THE TRAITORS MOVE TO UNDERMINE

Clay's success in consolidating the Union-Russian alliance produced more than a mild panic in London, and the British Fifth Column in the U.S. government, their agents of influence, actively lobbied Lincoln for Clay's recall and replacement. Ironically, a positive governmental shift accomplished by Lincoln, the removal of Simon Cameron as Secretary of War on the grounds of rank incompetence, was to become the object of a "double judo" by the Fifth Column.

At one stroke, and most unfortunately, Lincoln was effectively persuaded by Seward et al. to replace Cameron with the notorious traitor Edwin Stanton as Secretary of War, while Cameron was shunted off to become the new U.S. ambassador to Russia, replacing Clay. This all occurred in the spring of 1862. Clay was bitter over the move, and begged Lincoln to allow his nephew, who had accompanied him as his assistant, to succeed him. In simple shorthand that meant: "Don't entrust the fate of the vital entente to anyone outside the Carey network." Despite these protests, Clay was recalled, leaving St. Petersburg in June 1862, the same month in which Cameron arrived.

Clay fought these dirty maneuvers tooth and nail, pointing out to Lincoln that the purpose of appointing Cameron to St. Petersburg was to ensure no effective American presence and communication with the Russian government during the most critical phase of the Civil War. Clay wrote to Lincoln in June 1862: "I had made arrangements to stay here and made the necessary expenditures accordingly. I have several thousands of roubles of property here, which is usually turned over to successors--but Mr. Cameron cannot buy: *He says he will positively ask leave to retire from this post at the end of the next quarter,* the 1st of September next. He proposes to come home on your leave of absence, and then remain" [emphasis added].

This letter makes clear how transparent the traitors' maneuver was: get Clay out, put in Cameron as a rump, three-month ambassador-in-name-only, and then leave the U.S.-Russian entente severed during precisely the phase of Civil War in which the danger of overt British military intervention was greatest.

Two things were to deny the British-agent conspirators the fruit of these evil schemes. Clay, though losing the recall battle, was to return in short stead to St. Petersburg, as we shall see, and, more importantly, even during the critical non-Clay interregnum, Gorchakov and the American faction in Russia did not budge from their policies--despite a crescendo of activities by Britain's Russian agents-of-influence throughout 1862. The Russians, too, had their Stantons, their British faction surrounding the Czar, as Lincoln was surrounded. The Czar and Gorchakov, like Lincoln, never wavered.

Clay fought back. Denied for the time being the ambassadorship, Clay used the period of his return to the United States to organize nationwide public support for the entente with Russia, and for immediate emancipation of the slaves.

Upon arriving in Washington, D.C., Clay gave Lincoln a blunt strategic briefing on the European situation: "All over Europe governments are ready to intervene in America's affairs and recognize the independence of the Confederate States." Clay argued that "only a forthright proclamation of emancipation" and alliance with Russia "will block these European autocracies." In a speech at Odd Fellows' Hall in Washington, D.C., Clay began his public speaking tour for the consummation of the U.S.-Russian entente.

> I think that I can say without implications of profanity or want of deference, that since the days of Christ himself such a happy and glorious privilege has not been reserved to any other man to do that amount of good; and no

man has ever more gallantly or nobly done it than Alexander II, the Czar of Russia. I refer to the emancipation of 23,000,000 serfs. Here then fellow citizens, was the place to look for an ally. Trust him; for your trust will not be misplaced. Stand by him, *and he will, as he has often declared to me he will, stand by you.* Not only Alexander, but his whole family are with you, men, women and children [emphasis added].[40]

Clay's sane and clearcut policy of utilizing "to the hilt" the strategic options available to the Union to forestall English-French armed intervention, was readily accepted by Lincoln in both areas, movement towards emancipation, and securing the Russian alliance. Lincoln immediately commissioned Clay to sound out public opinion in his native border state of Kentucky on emancipation, as a test case, before applying the policy nationally. The President also authorized Clay to draft plans to restore Florida to the Union by armed colonization, to effect an important political signal to register both at home and abroad that the secessionist tide was ebbing, and that the Union was on the road to restoration.[41]

Clay resumed his speaking tour not as an individual, but as a sanctioned representative of Lincoln's express policy thrust. His opening speech on emancipation was delivered in the Kentucky state capital of Frankfort: "If fall we must, let us fall with the flag of universal liberty and justice nailed to the masthead . . . . The President's Florida plan of armed colonization is highly practical . . . . What can be done in Florida can be done in Texas and other Slave States."[42]

It was now dawning on Stanton, Seward and the Fifth Column that their coup in removing Clay from the ambassadorship was backfiring. Clay, in the United States, with constant personal access to Lincoln, was a far more dangerous adversary than Clay in St. Petersburg--very dangerous to the British faction as that location for Clay indeed was. Clay had effectively boxed in the "clever" Seward. Seward could have his choice of two distasteful options, keep Clay in the United States, or maneuver to get him "back to Russia." Swallowing bitterly, Seward chose the latter.

Seward advised Lincoln that Clay's speaking activities were "dangerous," that his "unrestrained agitation for emancipation will drive Kentucky into joining the secessionist States."[43] Lincoln accepted this "advice" to mend shaky domestic political fences, and, as Cameron's resignation as ambassador to Russia had just occurred, promptly reappointed Clay to his ambassadorship. Clay wrote an immediate acceptance letter to Lincoln:

> I avail myself of your kind promise to send me back to my former mission to the Court of St. Petersburg and where I flatter myself that I can better serve my country than in the field under General Halleck who cannot repress his hatred of liberal men into the ordinary courtesies of life.[44]

Then followed a tactical suggestion for Lincoln to further cement U.S.-Russian ties:

> The 1,000[th] anniversary of Russia's national existence is being celebrated there with great pomp and ceremony. In view of the Emperor's

known expressions of sympathy for the cause of the Union, would it not be well to write him an autograph letter of congratulation?[45]

Seward did not give up in his persistent efforts to remove Clay from the picture altogether. Seward's fallback now was to try to prevent Clay's confirmation by the Senate. Seward orchestrated a slander campaign to the effect that Clay was "persona non grata" to the Russian government. The widespread circulation of these lies succeeded in arousing significant opposition in the Senate against Clay's confirmation in his post. Clay, as in every other instance, took the matter head on, and in his writings and public statements made no secret of the fact that Seward was the architect of the campaign to "destroy the entente" by removing Clay.

Clay's counterattack began with the following letter to Lincoln;

> I am informed that the Committee of Foreign Relations will report against me on the ground that I am unacceptable to the Russian government. It is a false allegation. I can show more evidences of the good feeling of the Russian Court than any Minister there . . . I have letters at home of the most flattering kind from Prince Gorchakov before and since my arrival here. Baron de Stoeck1 (the Russian ambassador to the United States] called on me today and says if you will send for him he would make a most favorable report of me.
>
> Please send for him [de Stoeckl] and write to the Committee who takes the vote in the morning. Don't allow me to be slaughtered by

THE PERPLEXED PIRATES

LOUIS NAPOLEON [*a Corsair*]. "Vell, Meestare Jonnibull! vat you see zat time you peep round ze cornare tro your beeg glass?"

JOHN BULL [*Another*]. "I see a werry suspicious looking cove a sittin' in the New York 'arbor, with arf-a-dozen big Rooshian blood-hounds about him."

LOUIS NAPOLEON. "Hein?"

JOHN BULL. "Humph!"

From Harper's Weekly, *October 1863.*

a calumny. I have stood by you in good and evil report, and hope you will see justice done me.[46]

Lincoln and Clay triumphed, though after some delay in the confirmation proceedings.

Seward did not give up in his sabotage attempts even after Clay was confirmed. Under Cameron, a close crony of Seward's, Bayard Taylor, was appointed Secretary of the United States' Legation in St. Petersburg. Seward now demanded that Clay surrender the normal ambassadorial prerogative of naming his own Legation secretary, and retain Taylor. Taylor, before Lincoln had outflanked Seward and renominated Clay, had been Seward's handpicked choice to succeed Cameron. Our further description of Taylor will come from his own pen, a letter he wrote to a friend in Philadelphia during the Clay-Seward battle over the staffing of the St. Petersburg post:

> On the other hand, a man [Clay] who made the legation a laughing stock, whose incredible vanity and astonishing blunders are still the talk of St. Petersburg, and whose dispatches disgrace the State Department that allows them to be printed, will probably be allowed to come back to his ballet girls (his reason for coming) by our soft-hearted Abraham Lincoln.[47]

The "vain, blundering" Clay and "our softhearted Abraham Lincoln" promptly torpedoed the Seward-Taylor machinations. Clay chose Henry Bergh as his secretary and then drafted a long letter to Lincoln:

> Secretary of State Seward has ordered me to set off to St. Petersburg and leave the subject of

> Secretary of legation--there was already one at
> that place . . . I have asked Bayard Taylor if
> he were interested in remaining as Secretary of
> legation and he has peremptorily declined. Yet
> Mr. Seward accuses me of treating B. Taylor
> badly, by asking my legal rights of a Secretary.
> You see all this is merely a pretext to insult me
> by insulting my friends. Mr. Henry Bergh is a
> descendant of American ancestors of
> revolutionary fame: is a man who speaks most
> of the modern, languages--is an author-- and in
> every way my or Mr. Seward's equal. Yet he
> [Seward] is insulted because I ask his
> appointment. The custom in all Europe is for
> the Minister to appoint his secretary--for the
> most obvious reasons. It has always been the
> custom in this country. I feel that I have this
> right.[48]

Clay was adamant that there could be no compromise
on the life and death question for the Union in securing the
alliance with Russia, and the key to no compromising
meant keeping Seward and his lieutenants out of the most
critical diplomatic negotiations in United States history.
Clay's next letter to Lincoln made Lincoln further aware of
Seward's sabotage of the Clay mission--the already cited
Taylor maneuver, and the outright denial of Department
funds for Clay's and the mission's expenses in St.
Petersburg.

> It wouldn't be just to have a Seward spy in my
> house. I name Wm. H. Bergh as my Secretary
> and no other can render me any service. If a
> Sewardite is thrust upon me I shall regard it as
> an unfriendly act on your part . . . the rebels
> [Confederate cavalry guerrilla raids on
> Kentucky] have ruined my already poor means

of living by their continuous raids .   .   .   .
Now Seward is delaying his letter of credit, and
I am unable to receive a civil response from the
Department of State. Mr. Lincoln, I am poor
but honest. You have given me an office. I
have discharged it faithfully and to the interest
of my country--treat me justly .   .   .   . I grieve
to trouble you with this matter, or any matter.
But I am not master of my own movements. I
am in the hands of men who seek my ruin. I
ask your protection.[49]

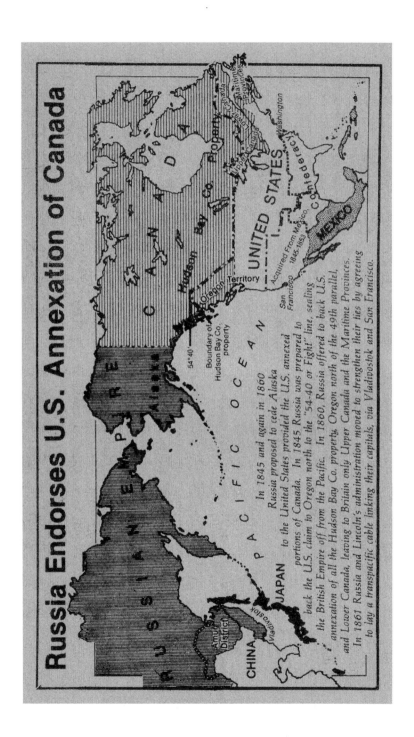

Russia Endorses U.S. Annexation of Canada

In 1845 and again in 1860 Russia proposed to cede Alaska to the United States provided the U.S. annexed portions of Canada. In 1845 Russia was prepared to back the U.S. claim to Oregon north to the "54-40 or Fight" line, sealing the British Empire off from the Pacific. In 1860, Russia offered to back U.S. annexation of all the Hudson Bay Co. property, Oregon north of the 49th parallel, and Lower Canada, leaving to Britain only Upper Canada and the Maritime Provinces. In 1861 Russia and Lincoln's administration moved to strengthen their ties by agreeing to lay a transpacific cable linking their capitals, via Vladivostok and San Francisco.

RUSSIA SAVES THE UNION

During Clay's absence from St. Petersburg from June 1862 until the spring of 1863, there was no wavering of Russia's support for the Union. United States Secretary of War Cameron arrived in St. Petersburg in June 1862 with instructions from Lincoln to secure an interview with the Czar to "learn the Russian monarch's attitude in the event England and France forced their unwelcome intervention." After the interview, Cameron was able to report to Lincoln:

> The Czar's spokesmen have assured me that in case of trouble with the other European powers, the friendship of Russia for the United States would be shown *in a decisive manner which no other nation will be able to mistake* [emphasis added].[50]

Cameron wrote the following on the Russian political situation to Secretary of State Seward in July, 1862.

> The Russians are evincing the most candid friendship for the North . . . . They are showing a constant desire to interpret everything to our advantage. There is no capital in Europe where the loyal American meets with such universal sympathy as at St. Petersburg, none where the suppression of our unnatural rebellion will be hailed with more genuine satisfaction.[51]

Already by the Civil War's summer 1862 campaigns, every knowledgeable leading political figure in Europe and the United States alike was drawing only one conclusion from the message which Cameron conveyed from the Czar to Lincoln: that foreign intervention in the American Civil

War in support of the Confederacy would be taken as a *casus belli* by Russia.

Seward understood the implications of the Czar's message immediately, and on June 25, 1862 hastily drafted the following letter to John Bigelow, the United States Consul in Paris, instructing him to inform the governments of Europe of what they could expect should they intervene.

> Between you and myself alone, I have a belief that the European state, whichever one it may be, that commits itself to intervention anywhere in North America, will sooner or later fetch up in the arms of a native of an oriental country not especially distinguished for amiability of manners of temper . . . . It might be well if it were known in Europe that we are no longer alarmed by demonstrations of interference.[52]

The autumn of 1862 was extremely critical for the Union. England and France were on the verge of military intervention on the side of the Confederacy. On the Union side, everyone from Lincoln on down was girding for what all believed was the "inevitable" Anglo-French invasion, an invasion which could include British allies Spain and Austria as well. Anglo-French pressure on Russia to abandon its pro-Union stance was stepped up to fever pitch. The Union's salvation depended on Russia.

This is no mere cliche. Lincoln, in this darkest hour of his Administration, sent an urgent personal letter to Russian Foreign Minister Gorchakov for delivery to the Czar.[53] Lincoln believed correctly that France had already decided to intervene and was only awaiting a go-ahead from England. England was expected to join France in the intervention. Lincoln was under absolutely no illusions that if the Union was to be saved, it would be saved by Russia. And Russia came through.

We quote here in full Foreign Minister Gorchakov's reply to the President, drafted in the name of Czar Alexander II. It is one of the most critical documents in American and world history.

> You know that the government of United States has few friends among the Powers. England rejoices over what is happening to you; she longs and prays for your overthrow. France is less actively hostile; her interests would be less affected by the result; but she is not unwilling to see it. She is not your friend. You situation is getting worse and worse. The chances of preserving the Union are growing more desperate. Can nothing be done to stop this dreadful war? The hope of reunion is growing less and less, and I wish to impress upon your government that the separation, which I fear must come[54] will be considered by Russia as one of the greatest misfortunes. Russia alone, has stood by you from the first, and will continue to stand by you. We are very, *very* anxious that some means should be adopted-- that *any* course should be pursued--which will prevent the division which now seems inevitable. One separation will be followed by another; you will break into fragments [emphasis original].[55]

The world historical interchange continued, with Bayard Taylor, Secretary of the Legation to St. Petersburg, acting under Lincoln's instructions, giving the United States reply:

We feel that the Northern and Southern States cannot peacefully exist side by side as separate republics. There is nothing the American people desire so much as peace, but peace on the basis of separation is equivalent to continual war. We have only just called the whole strength of the nation into action. We believe the struggle now commencing will be final, and we cannot without disgrace and ruin, accept the only terms tried and failed.[56]

Gorchakov reiterated Russia's stance, giving Taylor the following message to convey to Lincoln.

You know the sentiments of Russia. We desire above all things the maintenance of the American Union as *one indivisible nation.* We cannot take any part, more than we have done. We have no hostility to the Southern people. Russia has declared her position and will maintain it. There will be proposals of intervention [by Britain]. We believe that intervention could do no good at present. *Proposals will be made to Russia to join some plan of interference.* She will refuse any intervention of the kind. Russia will occupy the same ground as at the beginning of the struggle. *You may rely upon it, she will not change.* But we entreat you to settle the difficulty. I cannot express to you how profound an anxiety we feel--how serious are our fears [emphasis original].[57]

How many Americans today know that Russia intervened at this October 1862 darkest hour of the American Republic to save it, as the above-cited proceedings conclusively establish? But every living

American citizen--indeed all informed citizens of the world--at that time knew in full the official Russian reply to Lincoln, as conveyed by Gorchakov in his interview to Taylor.

In fact, the entire proceedings were ordered published and distributed throughout the nation by a joint resolution of Congress.[58]

The timing of the Russian reply was perfect. It followed by days the delivery to the United States government of Petit Napoleon's proposal for an armistice (a prelude to intervention), conveyed by the French Minister in Washington. "An armistice for six months, during which time every act of war, direct or indirect, should provisionally cease on the sea as well as on land, and it might be if necessary, ulteriorly prolonged."[59] It was obvious to all concerned that this proposal for a so-called armistice was an ultimatum to Lincoln to stop prosecuting the war and revoke the Union's naval blockade of the Confederacy. In short, it was a proposal to render permanent the split in the Union.

The gravity of the situation can be readily documented from hundreds of sources. Lincoln's secretaries, Nicolay and Hay commented thus:

> Many years elapsed before it became generally known how near the British government had come to accepting or even anticipating the overtures of France for mediation. On the 17th of October 1861, Lord John Russell had proposed a somewhat peremptory summons to the North and South to make up their quarrel, but Palmerston had not thought it advisable. In

September, 1862 Lord Palmerston himself revived the proposition in a note to Lord Russell, who was in attendance on the Queen at Gotha. Lord Russell at once gave his adhesion to the scheme. "I agree with you," he said, "that the time is come for offering mediation to the United States government with a view to the recognition of the independence of the Confederates. I agree further that, in case of failure, we ought to ourselves recognize the Southern States as an independent state." Lord Palmerston answered in the same vein.[60]

There is no better source than the words of Lord Russell himself to prove that the only consideration forestalling British intervention against the forces of the Union was the question: "What will Russia do?" A few days after the cited Russell-Palmerston agreement on intervention was reached, Russell wrote to Palmerston expressing second thoughts:

My only doubt is whether we and France should stir if Russia holds back. Her separation from our move would ensure the rejection of our proposals.[61]

The British cabinet was now plunged into the crucial debate on whether to Intervene, with all eyes and ears nervously awaiting the signal from St. Petersburg of what Russia's response to Britain's overtures would be. In the midst of the debate, Lord Russell received a telegram from British Ambassador Napier in St. Petersburg advising him that Russia had rejected Napoleon's proposal of joint intervention. Russian Foreign Minister Gorchakov drafted the communique conveying the rejection to Napoleon III:

> It is essential to avoid the appearance of any
> pressure of a nature to offend American public
> opinion, and to excite susceptibilities very
> easily amused at the bare idea of intervention.
> Russia stands in peculiarly friendly relations
> with the United States and cannot see its way
> clear to join a European coalition to interfere in
> American affairs.[62]

Russell read this, and, bitterly enraged but keeping a stiff upper lip, jotted a note to Palmerston: "We ought not to move at present without Russia."[63]   On November 13, after heated and bitter debate, the British cabinet reached its decision on the reply to Napoleon's proposals: "It is the cabinet's belief that there exists no ground at the moment to hope that Lincoln's government would accept the offer of mediation . . . ."[64]

One can almost hear Russell muttering, "Foiled this time, we'll get them next around."

To deliver the final blow to the purveyors of historical fraud and their investment banker masters, who have conspired to rob the American and Russian populace of the history of the great United States-Russian entente, we grant the final word to Czar Alexander II, who, among other things, held sole power to declare war for Russia:

> In the Autumn of 1862, the governments of
> France and Great Britain proposed to Russia, in
> a formal but not in an official way, the joint
> recognition by European powers of the
> independence of the Confederate States of
> America. My immediate answer was: "I will
> not cooperate in such action; and I will not
> acquiesce. On the contrary, I shall accept the

recognition of the independence of the Confederate States by France and Great Britain as a *casus belli* for Russia. And in order that the governments of France and Great Britain may understand that this is no idle threat; 1 will send a Pacific fleet to San Francisco and an Atlantic fleet to New York."

Sealed orders to both Admirals were given. My fleets arrived at the American ports, there was no recognition of the Confederate States by Great Britain and France. The American rebellion was put down, and the great American Republic continues.

All this I did because of love for my own dear Russia, rather than for love of the American Republic. I acted thus because I understood that Russia would have a more serious task to perform if the American Republic, with advanced industrial development were broken up and Great Britain should be left in control of most branches of modern industrial development.[65]

This statement was made on August 17, 1879 in an interview granted by the Czar to the American banker Wharton Barker. Barker at the time was the official financial agent of the Russian government in the United States, having been appointed in 1878 by the Grand Duke Constantine.[66]

THE CONSUMMATION Of THE ENTENTE

British-inspired historiography has run itself ragged trying to explain away the Czar's statement as an "after-the-fact boast," "spurious," and so on. Despite these howls from the anglophiles of the academic world, the statement is accurate. Every facet of this analysis of Russian policy during the Civil War period coheres with the first-hand historical evidence of the period, from both American and Russian sources.

Not even the most wretched of the liberal rewriters of history dares dispute the points made here concerning the Anglo-French proposal to Russia for joint intervention to recognize and support the Confederacy--the documentation from the mouths of Lords Russell and Palmerston is far too overwhelming--and the Czar's total rejection of that proposal.   Rather, the historical nitpicking disputes the Czar's use of the terms "casus belli'" and "sealed orders" for the fleet.[67] We shall return to this point in short order, after first occupying ourselves briefly with the concluding portion of this historic interview.

Was the Czar's statement--"I acted thus because I understood that Russia would have a more serious task to perform if the American Republic, with advanced industrial development were broken up and Great Britain should be left in control . . ." -- "boastful afterthought"?

What the liberal anglophile historians so fraudulently "overlook"--to use the polite word for cover-up--is that this concluding section of the interview is 100 percent consistent with the internal industrial development policy for Russia ardently fostered by Alexander II. This industrialization policy-thrust was consciously modeled on American Hamiltonian dirigism. Once this is understood, the liberal linguistic game-playing on such issues as "what did United States 'democracy' and Russian 'autocracy' have in common" is cut through like the proverbial Gordian knot.

The outlook of the Russian "American Faction" was expressly to emulate the United States as the model for industrial development. But they were operating under aggravating conditions of mass cultural deprivation and illiteracy that contrasted as night to day with the conditions prevailing in the American Republic. That hideous complication in the Russian situation was the basis on which British factioneers among the nobility and governmental strata were to continually abort and contain Russia's strides towards industrial development. Nevertheless, the emulation of the American System by the Russian "Whigs" was acted on in a most profound manner during the Civil War period.

Contrary to general mythology, the emancipation of the serfs was not a one-shot deal with no follow-up. The emancipation was undertaken consciously to remove the primary social obstacle to Russia's industrialization. The emancipation coincided with Russia's initiation of a massive railroad building program, itself conceived as the infrastructural precondition to industrialization.

In 1862, the model of American dirigism was the hegemonic concept guiding Russian policy. In that year a State Bank was created for the purpose of extending credit to develop commerce and industry. Even before the American Civil War, the Czar had extended the principle of the American model to the reequipping of his navy with ships of American design and importing technologically superior American-made cannon for the fleet.

As to the *casus belli* matter, the nitpicking here is extraordinary. The hue and cry from the liberals is a primeval scream; "He never said more than 'decisive manner.' " This, then is the pathetic Fabian fallback position, for in order to do more than nitpick, they are forced to deny the historical validity of the statements of not just one head of state, but of two.

We have the Czar's statement on record, now we may cite Lincoln. Lincoln confided to Senator Harlan in late 1862 that he had inquired as to the Czar's attitude should England and France militarily intervene against the Union. Lincoln told Harlan that the Czar had replied through the United States Minister Cameron that "in such a case the friendship of Russia for the United States will be shown in a decisive manner."[68]

THE RUSSIAN NAVY ARRIVES

The second half of 1863 and early 1864 mark the second critical phase of the Civil War period, where again the world came very close to a British-instigated eruption of global shooting war. As opposed to the late 1862 conjuncture, when the British were scheming intervention on the basis of the Confederacy's political high-water mark, the latter half of 1863 witnessed even more earnest British deliberations on intervening, this time on a now-or~never basis.

By mid-July 1863, psychotic desperation gripped Lords Russell and Palmerston. The South's invasion of the North had failed at Gettysburg. The synchronously timed violent antiwar movement in the North, including the bloody New York City draft riots, had also failed. As of July 4, 1863, the Union controlled the entire length of the Mississippi, cutting the Confederacy in two, while the blockade had become almost completely effective. In Russia, the British-orchestrated Polish rebellion was being extinguished. The British grand strategy of balkanizing both the United States and the Russian Empire and creating the satrapial "United States of Europe" was crumbling into dust.

In these utterly desperate circumstances, Britain was crazy enough to go to war, and almost did. Throughout the summer of 1863, repeated thinly disguised ultimatums were hurled at Russia by Britain and France on "the Polish question," threatening war. Simultaneously, the British were deliberating on intervening against the Union.[69]

War almost came in the late summer and fall of 1863. The fact that it did not was not a result of British policy in and of itself, but because resolute joint U.S.-Russian war preparations and preemptive actions raised the penalty factor to a threshold sufficient to force Britain once again to withdraw from the brink.

It was in this context that the entire Russian Navy arrived in the United States on September 24, 1863.

The dispatching of the Russian fleet to United States waters reflected a Russian policy decision made before the receipt of the British-French ultimatum on the Polish question. The receipt of the ultimatum merely made operational what was Russian policy from the day the Civil War began.

Russia's policy from 1861 on was war avoidance as long as Britain did not intervene militarily against the Union. From 1861, Russia developed a war-fighting strategy in the event Britain could not be dissuaded from intervening. One critical strategic aspect of this contingency plan concerned the deployment of the Russian fleet.

To avoid a repetition of the disaster of the Crimean War, where the fleet was bottled up and attacked in the Baltic and Black Seas, Russia's navy was placed on constant alert status during the United States Civil War, ready to set sail and head for the United States to join up with the United States Navy and provide a maximum combined naval capability that would be directed against the highly vulnerable island state of Britain. The timing of the fleet's departure from Russian ports was decided on the basis of highly accurate Russian intelligence estimates that considered the outbreak of war to be imminent. These estimates cohered with the fact that Britain's propensity to go to war in late 1863--given the desperation we have cited--was far greater than even during the intervention proposal period of late 1862.

The fleet that came on September 24, 1863 to United States waters--on both coasts simultaneously--came under arrangement of a United States-Russian political-military alliance which would become fully activated in the event of war. Cassius Clay, during his tenure as United States Ambassador to Russia, spoke openly and continuously of a

United States-Russian alliance.   No ambassador, without being subject to immediate recall,' could do such a thing if such an alliance did not actually exist.   Russian Foreign Minister Gorchakov also announced officially, in a communication to his ambassador, Stoeckl, that the alliance existed:

> I have given much thought to the possibility of concluding a formal political alliance .   .   . but that would not change anything in the existing position of the two nations .   .   . the alliance already exists in our mutual interests and traditions.[70]

To this memo, dated October 22, 1863, Alexander II added the comment, "tres bien."[71]

The existence of the alliance and the famous "sealed orders" cannot be disputed.   The testimony of both the United States and Russian Navy commanders exists to fully corroborate Czar Alexander II's assertion.   Lincoln confidante Thurlow Weed related this on the basis of a conversation with the Union Commander, Admiral Farragut:

> Admiral David Farragut lived at the Astor House, where he was visited frequently by the Russian admiral, between whom, when they were young officers serving in the Mediterranean, a warm friendship had existed. Sitting in Thurlow Weed's room one evening after dinner, Admiral Farragut said to his Russian friend: "why are you [the fleet] spending the winter here .   .   .?"   "I am here, replied the Russian admiral, under sealed orders, to be broken only in a contingency that has not occurred."   He added that the Russian

men-of-war were lying off San Francisco with similar orders. During this conversation, the Russian admiral admitted that his orders were to break the seals if, during the rebellion, we [the United States] became involved in a war with foreign nations.[72]

The testimony of Governor Andrew Curtin of Pennsylvania, Clay's successor as ambassador to Russia and, like Clay, a confidant of Gorchakov's, is even more explicit. Curtin publicly stated that during his tenure as ambassador Gorchakov showed him three letters. The first was that of Napoleon III inviting the Czar to join France and England in recognition of the Confederacy; the second was the Czar's letter to Napoleon III, declining the invitation and pledging that Russia would give active aid to the United States if the other powers attempted to intervene; the third contained the sealed orders to the Russian commander, Admiral Lessovsky to place his fleet at the command of the President of the United States in the event of war.[73]

The United States admirals, the Russian admirals, the Czar, Clay, and as we shall see, the press here, all spoke in terms of alliance, "sealed orders," and so on. The British and French hysterically denounced the United States-Russian alliance. Small wonder that the revisionist historians had to wait a full fifty years after the conclusion of the Civil War, to write the "definitive" refutation of the alliance. Even smaller wonder that the primary means of the historical fraud against the entente is simply to black it out completely from the United States population. We again return to our rhetorical question: How many Americans know at all that such an alliance ever existed?

In late 1863, the arrival and stay of the Russian Fleet in American waters was the lead story in the United States press and on everyone's lips, for months on end, relegating even the war coverage to second place on many a day.

PAVEL IVANOVICH JONES

The actual history of United States-Russian military-technological collaboration makes a mockery of the revisionists' fuss. The origins of the modern Russian Navy itself attest to this. John Paul Jones, or "Pavel Ivanovich Jones" as he was called during his service in the Russian Navy, did not "miraculously" arrive in Russia in 1788 and receive a commission as a rear admiral in Catherine the Great's navy. Nor was it mere chance that a document drafted by Jones in 1791, following his Russian tenure of duty, was adopted by Russia as the basis for reorganizing its fleet into a modern navy.[74]

From 1781 on, Princess Catherine Dashkov, the head of the Russian Academy of Sciences (of the same Dashkov family that Cassius Clay frequently cites as "my good friends" in his *Memoirs*) was in correspondence with Benjamin Franklin and his great-nephew and Paris secretary, Jonathan Williams--the future superintendent of West Point who is revered as the father of the United States Army Corps of Engineers. Dashkov functioned then and later as a liaison channeling Franklin's and Williams's political, scientific, and military writings into the Russian Naval Ministry and the Russian Academy of Sciences, where they were promptly translated and circulated. It was through similar network arrangements among leading figures that Alexander Hamilton's "Report on

Manufactures" was translated and widely circulating in Russia by 1793.[75]

In the period of Whig resurgence, beginning in the 1840s, the strong military-naval centered ties connecting the United States and Russia were refashioned. It was former Army Corps of Engineers officers who supervised the construction of Russia's first railroad. The individuals who were to become the Naval Commanders of both powers during the Civil War were already committed in their own minds to the policy of entente between the two powers based on their mutual commitment to progress no later than the Crimean War years. In the extensive fraternization and discussion that occurred among the Mediterranean squadron commanders (Farragut, the Grand Duke Constantine, Lessovsky, and others), a powerful United States-Russian military alliance against Great Britain came to be viewed by the participants as a historical necessity.

After the Civil War began, the implementation of a joint United States-Russian naval build-up began. Long before the Russian fleet was en route to the United States, a vast "intangible" stream of American military aid had already begun transforming Russia into a first-rate naval power, soon to be technologically superior to Great Britain. The abrupt transformation of "semi-barbarous" Russia into a first-class naval power was the subject of many fear-ridden commentaries in the London *Times*. In 1861, Russia still had no shipbuilding facilities for ironclads. By mid-1862, Cassius Clay's "Russian system" had not only established new shipyards capable of turning out ironclads (of the latest American designs, built to American specifications), but also the necessary metalworking, machine tool and armaments enterprises--all with completely indigenous materials and labor force.

The United States' military build-up of Russia was seen as precisely as the necessary military corollary to the development policies of the entente.   So it was taught to the cadets of the United States Naval Academy, as revealed from the long-suppressed writings of Professor Boynton, a key elite figure in his dual capacity as Professor at Annapolis and Chaplain to the United States House of Representatives:

> Since the Spring of 1862. Russia is actively engaged in enlarging her Navy. Like other nations, she has begun the construction of an ironclad fleet; like America's--comprised mainly at first of ships of the *Monitor* class--of which a number are already being built.
>
> The first necessity of Russia is precisely like our own. She needs batteries which will effectively protect her harbors against the ironclads of England and France; and at one-quarter cost of such ships as the *Warrior*, or the *Minotaur.* She can construct a Monitor battery that can demolish either of these.
>
> Russia has an unlimited supply of material for her Navy. Her shipyards are so situated that she can defend them against Europe; having also benefited of American experience and skills, [she] is able to construct a navy equal to any in the world.
>
> But the policy of Russia, like our own, demands peace and self-development, not war

and conquest; we both need means of defense that will keep our ambitious neighbors at home, and the means on the ocean of defending our growing commerce . . . .

   After the safety of our two nations has been cared for, the governments turn their attention to internal national development, and certainly no nation in the world can boast of a more enlightened, thorough, or scientific system of instruction than Russia herself has established . . . her great resources . . . agriculture, mines, her manufactures, her schools. And from "her schools as centers, an influence is diffused through the whole nations by which the resources of the Empire are sought out and developed by a combination of science and mechanical skill.[76]

By the end of the Civil War, Russia had thirteen ironclads, equipped with fifteen-inch guns, constructed from the blueprints of the *USS Passaic*--thirteen warships that nothing in the British Navy at the time was capable of sinking.[77]

1863 Draft Riots in New York City: part of Britain's last-ditch effort to save the Confederacy.

"GOD BLESS THE RUSSIANS"

On September 24, 1863, the Russian Fleet dropped anchor in New York harbor. America exploded with joy. The atmosphere of V-E Day can serve as a comparison for the emotional mood of the nation. Upon learning of the Fleet's arrival, Navy Secretary Gideon Welles wrote to the Russian Foreign Minister Gorchakov:

> The Department is much gratified to learn that a squadron of Russian war vessels is at present off the harbor of New York, with the intention of visiting that city. The presence in our waters of a squadron belonging to His Imperial Majesty's Navy cannot but be a source of pleasure and happiness to our countrymen. I beg that you will make known to the Admiral in command that the facilities of the Brooklyn Navy Yard are at his disposal for any repairs that the vessels of his squadron need, and that any other required assistance will be gladly extended.
>
> I avail myself of this occasion to extend through you to the officers of His Majesty's squadron a cordial invitation to visit that navy yard. I do not hesitate to say that it will give Rear Admiral Paulding very great pleasure to show them the vessels and other objects of interest at the naval station under his command.[78]

Welles wrote in his diary:

> In sending them to this country there is something significant. What will be its effect on France and the French policy we shall learn

in due time.   It may be moderate; it may
exasperate. God bless the Russians.

The press glowed with accounts of the Fleet.   *Harper's*
Weekly took special pride in pointing out the American
design of the ships and the armaments on board:

> The two largest of the squadron, the frigates
> A*lexander Nevski* and *Peresvet*, are evidently
> vessels of modern build, and much about them
> would lead an unpracticed eye to think they
> were built in this country .   .   .   .   The
> flagship's guns are of American make, being
> cast in Pittsburgh.[79]

The comparison to V-E day to illustrate the mood of the
United States' population is no exaggeration.   New York
City was "gaily bedecked with American and Russian
flags," the fleet's officers were given a special parade with
a United States' military honor guard escorting them up
Broadway past cheering crowds.   Here is *Harper's*
description of the parade, October 17, 1863:

> After the procession had passed Union Square
> and wheeling fairly into the vast current of
> Broadway, the scene became splendidly
> animated.   The moving pageant rolled in a
> glittering stream down the broad thoroughfare
> between banks of upturned human faces, the
> trappings of the equipages, the gold and silver
> epaulets of the Muscovite guests and the
> sabres, helmets and bayonets of the
> escort .   .   .   .   The cavalcade advanced to the
> joyous time of exulting martial music .   .   .
> and there was a proud and gratified feeling
> evident in the hearts of the vast concourse
> assembled to greet it, that would have been

befitting to the most important triumphs at home. Far as the eye could reach down the great central avenue of our imperial city, the sidewalks were packed with human beings, and the balconies and windows--nay, in some instances the very roofs of the buildings above them--were beset with eager multitudes . . . . Above nearly every building gayly fluttered the Stars and Stripes with scores of little Russian flags, waving side by side with our own national colors. By the way, it may be remarked that the great Autocracy and the great Republic had the scene all to themselves, no other nation being represented even in bunting--a significant incident of the ovation.[80]

The parade was but the beginning of an extended celebration including balls, galas, and other festivities. Delegations from many states poured into New York to extend gratitude to the Russians for their support of the Union. *Harper's* commented pointedly:

The ceremony was intended to have and had, a political significance . . . . Every citizen felt bound to do what in him lay to testify to the Russians our sense of gratitude for the friendly manner in which Russia has stood by us in our present struggle, while the Western Powers have done not a little to work our ruin.[81]

Harper's commentary was not unique. The patriotic American press all stressed the importance of the Russian Fleet's arrival and stay in United States' waters. *Harper's* summarized the "special significance" of Russia's naval support with this acerbic analysis of its possible consequences for Britain:

During the late Crimean War, the Russian Fleet was closely shut up at Kronstadt and in the Black Sea, and was unable to render any effective service. The Russians have now quite an effective naval force on the open seas. The experience of the *Alabama* and *Florida* [Confederate sea raiders] shows how much damage may be effected by one or two armed vessels upon the commerce of the enemy.

Should a war break out, as still seems most probable, between Russia and France and England, the example set by the English government will afford a precedent for our dealings with the belligerents. The Russian vessels now at large, with such aid as we can give, in precise accordance with the course of the English government toward us [the British, under the aegis of "neutrality," aided the Confederate raiders as far as practicable without an open declaration of belligerency against the Union], could render the commerce of England insecure.[82]

The existence of a de facto joint United States-Russian naval command and the threat such a combination could pose to Britain's maritime lifeline created an alarm and hysteria in Britain virtually without historical comparison. The combination of the two powers was the decisive factor in preventing war. The Russian fleet's arrival in United States waters "came as a shock to London." British newspapers began an angry howl, denouncing "Lincoln's threats of war" against Britain and launching a press campaign "poking fun" at the "Americans, who have been hoodwinked by the Russians."

Harper's Weekly ran an editorial in reply to this English psychological warfare campaign which expressed the prevailing consensus in the United States:

> John Bull thinks that we are absurdly bamboozled by the Russian compliments and laughs to see us deceived by the sympathy of Muscovy . . . . But we are not very much deceived. Americans understand that the sympathy of France in our Revolution for us was not for love of us, but from hatred of England. They know, as Washington long ago told them, that romantic friendship between nations is not to be expected. And if they had latterly expected it, England has utterly undeceived them.
>
> Americans do not suppose that Russia is on the point of becoming a Republic, but they observe that the English aristocracy and the French Empire hate a republic quite as much as the Russian monarchy hates it; and they remark that while the French Empire imports coolies into its colonies, and winks at slavery, and while the British government cheers a political enterprise founded upon slavery, and by its chief organs defends the system, Russia emancipates her serfs. There is not the least harm in observing these little facts. Russia, John Bull will remember, conducts herself as a friendly power. That is all. England and France have shown themselves to be unfriendly powers. And we do not forget it.[83]

The Russian Fleet was to remain in United States waters for seven months, departing in April 1864 only after both Russia and the United States had fully satisfied themselves that all danger of war from the Continent had passed. Throughout the stay there were continuous celebrations, festivities, and a daily public outpouring of American gratitude. The Russian ships stationed off New York sailed in December for Washington, D.C. and made their way up the Potomac River, dropping anchor at the nation's capital. This commenced another round of celebrations. With the unfortunate exception of Lincoln, who at the time was suffering a mild case of smallpox, the entire cabinet and Mrs. Lincoln hosted the Russian officers at gala receptions on board the flagship. The Russians toasted Lincoln, and Mrs. Lincoln led a toast to the Czar and the emancipation of the serfs.

A TWO-POWER, TWO-OCEAN NAVY

The Russian Pacific fleet's stay in San Francisco was also filled with celebrations, and provides further striking evidence of how detailed were the plans which had been worked out for the alliance.

During the Civil War the United States had only a one-ocean navy, and it patrolled the East Coast while the Pacific Coast remained unprotected by United States' naval forces. Under these conditions, the Russian fleet at San Francisco filled the wartime function of United States' Pacific fleet. Recall here the testimony of American Admiral Farragut and Russian Atlantic Fleet commander, Admiral Lessovsky, corroborating the Czar's reference to the existence of sealed orders for the Russian fleet's intervention on the side of the Union should England or her allies attack Lincoln's government. We now cite the testimony of Pacific Fleet commander Popov to establish the case that not only the Russian fleet in the Atlantic, but the Czar's Pacific fleet, as well, was under such orders.

In the winter of 1863-64, rumors swept San Francisco that an attack by the Confederate raiders *Alabama* and *Sumter* was imminent. The California government appealed to Admiral Popov for protection. Popov's reply, *citing his orders for the contingency of a British or a Confederate naval attack on the West Coast,* demonstrates beyond a doubt that London's continuous denunciations of a "secret alliance" between Russia and the United States during the Civil War period were the result of an hysteria based on strategic reality:

> Should a Southern cruiser attempt an assault . . . we shall put on steam and clear for action . . . . The ships of his Imperial Majesty are bound to assist the authorities of every place where friendship is offered them, in all measures which may be deemed necessary by the local authorities, to repel any attempt against the security of the place.[84]

The United States' West Coast was never attacked.

A final summary of the voluminous documentation of the existence of the United States-Russian military alliance attributing the salvation of the Union to the existence of the entente is now in order. We have cited the following primary sources: Russian Foreign Minister Gorchakov, Czar Alexander II, U.S. Ambassador to Russia Cassius M. Clay, Admiral Farragut, and Russian Fleet Commanders Lessovsky and Popov. Until the Fabian erasure job conducted in the early twentieth century, all post-Civil War accounts presented the alliance as a fact. Here we cite the

Union ironclad gunboats shelling Fort Henry on the Tennessee River in 1862. Both the decision to construct these ships and the plans for this offensive, under General U.S. Grant, were the work of Russian intelligence specialist Col. Charles DeArnaud.

account of United States Navy Commander F.E. Chadwick, corroborating Farragut and the others.

Chadwick confirms Pennsylvania Governor Andrew Curtin's report that Foreign Minister Gorchakov had shown Curtin a copy of the orders given to the Russian Admiral commanding the fleet sent to New York. The orders instructed the admiral, in the event of the recognition of the Confederacy by France or England, to place his fleet at the disposition of the American government. Popov's orders for the Pacific fleet, which we have quoted, said exactly the same thing. Chadwick summarized the contents of the alliance:

> In other words, the recognition [of the Confederacy by France or England] was to be the signal for the declaration by Russia of war against those powers. And there can be little doubt that the knowledge by the French and English cabinets of these orders was the great leash which held them in check.[85]

LINCOLN ON THE POLISH QUESTION

The entente was a two-way street. We have focused on the primary historical significance of the alliance: that the Union was saved as a result of Russia's unwavering support of the United States in the face of Britain's threats of invasion. The United States reciprocated in full, providing Russia a bulwark of political support--the sole one on the international scene--in the critical mid-to-late 1863 period when war seemed certain to be provoked by London's ultimatums on the British-created "Polish question."

The British position in this case was a historical paradigm of the application of the monetarists' "limited sovereignty" doctrine. The legal trapping of the doctrine was Britain's contention that under the terms of the Congress of Vienna, the "Powers" (i.e., Britain and its pawns on the Continent, in this case France's Petit Napoleon) had the "right" to impose a settlement--in this case, Polish secession--over the heads of the Russians in matters pertaining to the affairs of their own empire.

Lincoln saw the dangerous parallel in Britain's application of the Russell-Palmerston limited sovereignty doctrine against the Union. He was keenly aware of the crucial importance of Russia's explicit rejection of these British maneuvers, and the Czar's determination to go to war if necessary to ensure "one indivisible American nations." Lincoln cast aside all the Jacksonian-style "democracy, self-determination" advice thrust upon him, and rendered full Union support to Russian sovereignty and Russia's right to settle its own affairs, free of British interference. Lincoln and the Czar were in full principled agreement: at all costs, no allowance of a confederated America, and no allowance of a British satrapial "United States of Europe."

In May 1863, French Foreign Minister Drouyn de Lhuys invited Lincoln to join France, England, and Austria in an ultimatum against Russia in favor of the independence of "Poland." De Lhuys' proposal was doubly ironic. Obviously England was using the "Polish freedom" cry as the pretext to engineer war against Russia. But the sidelight of Austria piously joining Britain added the final touch of hypocrisy and fraud, considering the fact that the "freedom-loving" Hapsburgs ruled over one-third of former Poland. The invitation to the United States, was in effect an ultimatum to Lincoln to break his administration's alliance with Russia, or else. The text of de Lhuys' proposal ran as follows:

> The good relations which exist between the government of the United States and the court of Russia cannot but give greater weight to the counsels presented in a friendly form; and we rely entirely on the Cabinet in Washington to appreciate the measure in which it will be able most satisfactorily to open its views to the Russian government.[86]

Secretary of State Seward, long a foe of the United States-Russian entente, gobbled at the opportunity thus offered. Donning the Jacksonian toga, Seward "espoused the cause of Poland . . . that gallant nation whose wrongs, whose misfortunes and whose valor have so deeply excited universal sympathy in Europe." [87]

But Lincoln was not to be manipulated. His reply to de Lhuys was a curt statement of America's full confidence that "the Polish grievances shall be righted by the Sagacity and magnanimity of Czar Alexander II."

The anglophile press, here and abroad, villified Lincoln as never before. The *Missouri Republic*, linked to the wretched fraud Carl Schurz, waved the bloody shirt of Poland: "the pale corpse of Poland's murdered liberty shall haunt President Lincoln in the days to come." *Punch* magazine in England, in the characteristic English propaganda style of that time, depicted Lincoln conniving with a Russian bear. Petit Napoleon's French rags ran cartoons of Lincoln and Alexander with bloodied hands "sealing their Pact in blood," hysterically editorializing:

> Is it right that fifty million Muscovites should unite to retain ten or twelve million Poles under a detested yoke? . . . is it right that twenty million Northern Germans and Irishmen [i.e., the Union] unite to impose on eight million Southerners an association they spurn?[88]

Many were the hearty bellylaughs in the United States and Russia upon hearing the Anglo-French-Austrian chorus of "down with colonialism."

The Czar's appreciation of America's rejection of the Anglo-French ultimatum and firm support of Russia's sovereignty in its hour of need is documented in writing by Gorchakov, who, speaking for the Czar, praised

> . . . the firmness with which the government of the United States maintains the principle of nonintervention, the meaning of which in these days is so often perverted; as well as the loyalty with which they refuse to impose upon other states a rule, the violation of which, in respect to themselves if they will not allow. The federal government gives thus an example of justice and political propriety which must increase the esteem which our August Master has avowed toward the American nation . . .
> .

> His majesty, the Emperor, has been sensuously moved by the sentiments of confidence which the government of the United States places in his views and designs in regard to the general well-being of his Empire. Such

manifestation must strengthen the bonds of mutual sympathy which unite the two countries and constitute a consummation which too much accords with the aspirations of the Emperor, His Majesty, not to look upon it with pleasure.[89]

Ambassador Clay, in St. Petersburg, applauded Lincoln's consummation of the entente by reciprocating support for Russia: "It was due from us to be grateful for the past conduct of Russia toward us in our trouble, by a like moral support of herself, in defense of the integrity of her Empire." Clay coupled this with a scathing attack on the Lincoln advisors who counseled acceptance of Napoleon's invitation: "How could it help the United States to weaken our steadfast friend . . . . For should Russia suffer defeat it would open the way for our common enemies to fall upon us."

THE POSTWAR OUTLOOK

The central determinant of world politics through the period from 1863 to 1867 was the joint policy thrust of American Whigs and the Russian government to consolidate their wartime alliance into a permanent entente. The alliance was to have the immediate aim of containing British-sponsored evil around the globe, and the slightly longer-term goal of eliminating the British Empire to allow the unfettered emergence of a world community of republics. Throughout the 1860s, American and Russian "Whigs" continuously pushed to secure this permanent alliance, even, in the American case, under the enormous handicaps that emerged after Lincoln's assassination.

This campaign for permanent entente was no secret confined to "smoke-filled rooms." It was public, and immensely popular. It was the rallying cry in the foreign policy domain for all patriotic Americans during this period.

At the height of the celebration that engulfed the United States following the arrival of the Russian Fleet, on October 17, 1863, *Harper's Weekly* ran a milestone editorial which expressed the nation's ruling public sentiment. The editorial called for a permanent alliance with Russia, as the international strategic anchor to guarantee world peace and economic development for decades to come. This document speaks eloquently for itself:

> It seems quite doubtful, under these circumstances, whether we can possibly much longer maintain the position of proud isolation which Washington coveted . . . .
>
> The alliance of the Western Powers [Britain and France], maintained through the Crimean War and exemplified in the recognition of the Southern rebels by both powers conjointly--is in fact, if not in name, a hostile combination against the United States.
>
> What is our proper reply to this hostile combination? . . . Would it not be wise to meet the hostile alliance by an alliance with Russia? France and England united can do and dare much against Russia alone or the United States alone; but against Russia and the United States combined what could they do?

The analogies between the American and Russian people have too often been described to need further explanation here. Russia, like the United States, is a nation of the future. Its capabilities are only just being developed. Its national destiny is barely shaped. Its very institutions are in their cradle, and have yet to be modeled to fit advancing civilization and the spread of intelligence. Russia is in the agonies of a terrible transition: the Russian serfs like the American Negroes, are receiving their liberty; and the Russian boiars, like the Southern slaveowners, are mutinous at the loss of their property. When this great problem shall have been solved, and the Russian people shall consist of 100,000,000 of intelligent, educated beings, it is possible that Russian institutions will have been welded by the force of civilization into a similarity with ours. At that period, the United States will probably also contain 100,000,000 educated, intelligent people. Two such peoples, firmly bound together by an alliance as well as by traditional sympathy and good feeling, what would be impossible? Certainly the least of the purposes which they could achieve would be to keep the peace of the world . . . .

At the present time Russia and the United States occupy remarkably similar positions. A portion of the subjects of the Russian Empire, residing in Poland, have attempted to secede and set up an independent national existence, just as our Southern slaveowners have tried to secede from the Union and set up a slave Confederacy; and the Czar, like the government of the Union, has undertaken to put down the insurrection by force of arms. In that undertaking, which every government is bound to make under penalty of national suicide, Russia, like the United States has been thwarted and annoyed by the interference of France and England. The Czar, like Mr. Lincoln, nevertheless, perseveres in his purpose; and being perfectly in earnest and determined, has sent a fleet into our waters in order that, if war should occur, British and French commerce should not escape as cheaply as they did during the Crimean contest.

An alliance between Russia and the United States at the present time would probably relieve both of us from all apprehensions of foreign interference. It is not likely it would involve either nation in war. On the contrary, it would probably be the best possible guarantee against war. It would be highly popular in both countries . . . .

The reception given last week in this city to Admiral Lisovski and his officers will create more apprehension at the Tuilleries and at St. James than even the Parrott gun or the capture of the *Atlanta*. If it be followed up by diplomatic negotiations, with a view to an alliance with the Czar, it may prove an epoch of no mean importance in history.[91]

THE ENTENTE DECLINES . . .

The fact that such a post-Civil War epoch of peace and development, based on a formal "superpowers" entente, did not materialize, requires no long-winded explanations. Lincoln's assassination by a British conspiracy cost the United States Whigs the Executive. After Lincoln's death, the White House and the cabinet fell under the sway of British agents-of-influence, a political geometry that sealed the fate of the entente.

Treason at the top was the sole reason for the failure of the crucial Russian-American alliance. There were no legitimate-constituency-related domestic obstacles in the United States blocking the formation of a permanent entente. On the contrary, the idea of the permanent entente as the international strategic means to crush the British Empire was immensely popular. There were no problems of any consequence in the post-Civil War Republican Congress. In fact this Congress went on record as being emphatically "pro-Russian." On the Russian side, there were no obstacles of any consequence. The Czar was set on his pro-American course, and only a bullet could stop him.

The very probability that the entente would have been made permanent had not Britain intervened is made clear by the desperate character of Britain's deployments against the United States and Russia. The assassination of Lincoln did not spell the definite ending of the prospects for an entente. The British required "double insurance." A year and a day following Lincoln's death, on April 16, 1866 the Czar narrowly escaped assassination. Ambassador Clay met personally with the Czar shortly afterwards, to convey "warm congratulations" on his escape' from death, "so soon following Lincoln's murder." The Czar replied: "I trust under Providence that our mutual calamities will strengthen our friendly relations and render them permanent."[92]

News of the assassination attempt galvanized American Whigs into action. The Republican congressional leadership met and decided something "more solemn and tangible" than expressions of congratulations was in order. They drafted a joint resolution of the Congress, which was overwhelmingly passed, which authorized the sending of a special envoy to Russia, "to convey in person to His Imperial Majesty America's good will and congratulations to the twenty millions of serfs upon the providential escape from danger of the Sovereign to whose head and heart they owe the blessings of their freedom."[93]

The dynamic evident here ought to be obvious. The assassination attempt on the Czar provided a convenient pretext for the congressional leadership--thoroughly enraged and exasperated over the Administration's policy of "marking time" on vital foreign policy thrusts--to take further development of the entente with Russia into their own hands.

Assistant Secretary of the Navy Gustavus Vasa Fox was selected to head the mission, sailing on board the new naval ironclad, *Miantonomoh*. The mission, after stops in England, France, and Denmark, was scheduled to arrive in Kronstadt. The announcement of Fox's trip and its departure destabilized the British and the French as no event had since before Lincoln's death. At the French stopover, Fox had a private meeting with Emperor Napoleon III.

Napoleon began the talks with the announcement that he was "about to withdraw from his British-backed occupation of Mexico, a matter in which, as Fox well knew, he had no choice. In return for this magnanimous decision Napoleon merely requested of Fox that America conclude no alliance with Russia. This segment of the dialogue went as follows:

> Napoleon: "Do not be too friendly with Russia."

> Fox: "Russia and America have no rival interests. Russia has always been friendly to America and we reciprocate the feeling."

> Napoleon: "But you can stand alone. You do not want friends."

> Fox: "When it was doubtful whether we should ever stand again, at a time when the most powerful nations menaced us, Russia felt and expressed her sympathy for us, and America will never forget it." [94]

On Aug. 8, 1866, Fox, accompanied by Clay, formally presented the joint resolution of the Congress to Alexander II, with Russian Foreign Minister Gorchakov standing in attendance. Both the resolution and the Czar's reply (also sent as a letter to President Johnson) are here reproduced beginning with Fox's reading of the resolution;

> Sire: The Resolution which I have the honor of presenting to Your Imperial Majesty is the voice of a people whose millions of lips speak from a single heart.

> The many ties which have long bound together the great Empire of the East, and the great Republic of the West, have been multiplied and strengthened by the unwavering

fidelity of the imperial government to our own, throughout its recent period of convulsion.

The words of sympathy and friendship then addressed to the government at Washington, by command of your Imperial Majesty, are fixed in the eternal remembrance of a grateful country. As one of the wide family of nations, we yield our willing homage to that act of humanity which is especially referred to in the Resolution of Congress. The peaceful edict of an enlightened sovereign has consummated a triumph over an inherited barbarism, which our Western republic has only reached through long years of bloodshed.

. . . our heartfelt congratulations upon the providential escape from danger . . . and thankfulness for its merciful arrest and failure.

The story of the peril [the assassination attempt] . . . brings with it the remembrance of the mighty sorrow . . . at the loss of our chief, our guide . . . .

We thank God that a grief like this was spared to our friends and allies--the Russian people.[95]

The Czar's reply, read by Gorchakov:

His Majesty . . . rejoices at the friendly relations existing between Russia and the United States, and he is pleased to see that those relations are so well appreciated in America. He is convinced that the national fraternity will be perpetual, and be, for his part,

will contribute all his efforts to sustain it, and
to strengthen the bonds . . . .

　　. . . The mutual sympathy between Russia
and the United States is a consolatory fact in
the face of the recent complications which have
just awakened in Europe sentiments of hate,
ambition, rivalry, bloody struggles, appeals to
force, so little in harmony with the progress of
humanity . . . . The seeds of mutual good
will and friendship sown between two great
peoples will . . . inaugurate between them
relations founded on a real spirit of Christian
civilization.[96]

Even the Fabian historians concede: "these effusive
declarations revived conjectures, both in Europe and
America, as to the existence or imminence of a full~dress
Russian-American alliance."[97]

As America had done in 1863, now Russia celebrated as
the American delegation went on a national tour:

There were visits to the Kremlin, to palaces,
cathedrals and historic sites. There were
entertainments, fireworks, parades and
demonstrations in the streets everywhere the
Americans went. And everywhere they were
received with enthusiastic shouts and cheers.
The streets and public buildings were decorated
with shields bearing the portraits of
Washington, Lincoln, Johnson and Alexander
II, and the Stars and Stripes waved alongside of
the Russian national emblem. [98]

And everywhere, at every function, every speech,
Russian speakers delivered stiring eulogies to Lincoln, and

praise to America's striving to accomplish its "historical calling," on the principles of its founding fathers.

At this juncture the full scope of what could have been had Lincoln survived was filled out in a *New York Herald* commentary dated April 29, 1867:

> Russia and the United States, the young giants respectively of the Old and New Worlds, in whom are concentrated greater vitality and strength than in any other of the modern powers, are at this moment, although in most respects the antipodes of each other, engaged in the same work--that of expansion and progression. They stand now upon two continents, the one the impersonation of absolutism, the other of republicanism. No two nations bear at once a more forceful resemblance and exhibit a more striking contrast, and at this moment no two are watched with more solicitude and more likely to accomplish more stupendous results. The specific ultimate object at which Russia aims is the acquisition of the European possessions of the Sultan. With the proud city of Constantinople, the command of the Bosporus and the commerce of the Black Sea under her control, she would effectually be mistress of Europe. The United States do not define their aspirations but look quietly forward to the time the whole boundless continent will form one unbroken republic. The remarkable *entente cordiale* which for a quarter of a century has been increasing between us renders this similarity of object the most natural. Russia and the United States must ever be friendly, the colossi having neither territorial nor maritime jealousies to excite the one against the other.

The interests of both demand that they should
go hand in hand in their march to empire.[99]

. . . AND COMES TO AN END

The U.S. delegation's tour marked the postwar high-water mark of the Entente. After late 1866, the cabinet of the Johnson Administration, under Secretary of State Seward's direction, successfully implemented a containment strategy against the Whig goals. Under this setup, Seward's purchase of Alaska did not represent a breakthrough in United States-Russian relations. Rather, Seward did the minimum possible to satiate the Whigs. By doing nothing further to hit against Britain in either the Pacific or in Canada, as Clay and the Russians were demanding, Seward and Co. allowed the British to use both the Alaska sale and United States inertia to consolidate their position in Canada, one step in the restabilizing of British imperial hegemony on a global scale. The consolidation included the murder of Alexander II at the hands of a British-deployed assassin in March 1881.

Humanity, then, came very close to securing the world for global industrial development, with a United States-Russian entente as its strategic core. The prospects for entente and the objective capability of a United States-Russian alliance to finish off the City of London exist today. We dare not fail a second time.

Notes

1. *Proceedings of the American Philosophical Society*, 91:1947.

2. Clay, Cassius Marcellus, *The Life of Cassius Marcellus Clay, Memoirs, Writings and Speeches* (Cincinnati: J.F. Brennan and Co., 1886).

3. Adams, John Quincy, *Memoirs of John Quincy Adams*, Vol. 2.

4. Horton, Edward Everett, *Memoirs, Writings and Speeches of Edward Everett Horton.* See in particular Horton's speech at the 1864 Boston banquet in honor of the Russian fleet. Also, the speech of Russian Admiral Lessovsky, as summarized in the *Memoirs*.

5. *Ibid.*, including remarks by Admiral Lessovsky.

6. Callahan, James Morton, "Russo-American Relations During the American Civil War," Morgantown: *West Virginia University Studies in American History*, 1908, Series I, Diplomatic History Series Nos. 2 and 3.'

7. *Ibid.*

8. *Ibid.*

9. *Ibid.*

10. *Ibid.*

11. *Ibid.*

12. *Ibid.*

13. *Ibid.*

14. *Ibid.*

15. *Ibid.*

16. *Ibid* .

17. *Ibid.*

18. Clay, *The Life of Cassius Marcellus Clay.*

19. *Ibid.*

20. *Ibid.*

21. *Ibid.*

22. *Ibid.*

23. Lincoln Papers: No. 10880-4, Clay to Lincoln, private, July 25, 1861.

24. *Ibid.*

25. *Ibid.*

26. Diplomatic Correspondence of the United States in the Archives of the Department of State, June 21, 1861.

27. Adams, Ephraim Douglass, *Great Britain and the American Civil War* (Longmans, Green & Co., 1925).

28. The revisionist, anglophile, fraudulent rewriting of the history of the United States-Russian alliance begins in earnest after 1905. The most frequently

cited "authoritative" historians who constructed the "alliance was a myth" school, are Frank A. Golder and E.A. Adamov. The works that became the basis for interpretation of the period were Golder, Frank Alfred,' "The Russian Fleet and the Civil War," *American Historical Review* Vol. XX (1915), No. 4, pp. 801-812; by the same author, "The American Civil War through the Eyes of a Russian Diplomat," *American Historical Review* Vol. XXVI (1921), No. 3, pp. 454-463; and Adamov, E.A., "Russia and the United States at the Time of the Civil War," *Journal of Modern History* Vol. II (1930), pp. 582-602.

29. Thomas, Benjamin Platt, "Russo-American Relations, 1815-1867," *Johns Hopkins Studies,* series 48 (1930).

30. *Ibid.*

31. DeArnaud, Charles A., *The Union and Its Ally Russia* (Washington: Gibson Bros., 1890).

32. *Ibid.*

33. *Ibid.*

34. *Ibid.*

35. *Ibid.*

36. *Ibid*

37. *Ibid.*

38. *Ibid.*

39. *Ibid.*

40. Clay, *The Life of Cassius Marcellus Clay*.

41. *Ibid.*

42. *Ibid.*

43. *Ibid.*

44. *Ibid.*

45. *Ibid.*

46. *Ibid.* An important parenthetical note must be introduced here concerning the role of the Russian ambassador Baron; de Stoeckl. To the extent the Baron played a positive role, as in this instance, it was solely because, as a diplomat, he served under strict orders of Prince Gorchakov. orders which de Stoeckl could not "duck." De Stoeckl's actual role was to continuously draft situation reports on the United States, every one of which was a classic of faked intelligence in the British technique. These reports, conscious lies which completely distorted the United States' political situation along the lines of the London Times and Petit Napoleon's scribble sheets, were calculated to sway Russian policy away from Lincoln, and towards an accommodation with Lords Russell and Palmerston. That the veritable deluge of faked intelligence which swamped Gorchakov and the Czar during the Civil War totally failed, in net result, to achieve its' intended effect, constitutes ample grounds for tribute to the moral integrity of the American faction in Russia. Lied to, swindled, deceived, and manipulated, they never wavered in their

commitment to ensure the continued existence and prosperity of our country.

47. Taylor, Bayard, *Life and Letters*, edited by Marie Hansen Taylor and Horace E. Scudder (Boston: Houghton Mifflin Co., 1884).

48. Lincoln Papers, No. 22780-3, Clay to Lincoln, private, from New York, April 2, 1863.

49. Clay, *The Life of Cassius Marcellus Clay*.

50. Callahan, James, "Russo-American Relations During the American Civil War," Morgantown: *West Virginia University Studies in American History*, 1908, Series I, Diplomatic History No. 1.

51. Cameron to Seward, Dispatches, Russia, in U.S. Department of State Manuscripts, 1860-1869, Washington.

52. John Bigelow, *Retrospections of an Active Life*, Vol. 1, pp. 499-500.

53. Balch, Thomas W.   *The Alabama Arbitration* (Philadelphia: Allen, Lane and Scott, 1900).

54. The Czar's pessimism here concerning the Union's prospects for success reflects the quality of intelligence emanating from de Stoeckl.

55. Thomas, "Russo-American Relations, 1815-1867."

56. *Ibid.*

57. *Ibid.*

58. Adams, *Great Britain and the American Civil War*.

59. *Ibid.*

60. Nicolay, John G. and Hay, John, Abraham Lincoln: A History (New York: Century, 1890), Vol. 6, pp. 66-67.

61. Adams, *Great Britain and the American Civil War,* Vol. 2, p. 54.

62. *Ibid.*

63. *Ibid.*

64. *Ibid.*

65. Barker, Wharton, "The Secret of Russian Friendship," published in the *Independent,* LVI, March 24, 1904.

66. Hawkins, General Rush Christopher, "The Coming of the Russian Ships in 1863," N*orth American Review* Vol. 178 (1903). pp. 539-544.

67. Cf. note 28.

68. Nicolay and Hay, *Abraham Lincoln: A History,* Vol. 6.

69. Adams, *Great Britain and the American Civil War.* Vol. 2.

70. *Ibid.*

71. *Ibid.*

72. *Life of Thurlow Weed, Including his Autobiography* (2 vols., 1883-1884), Vol. 2, p. 346.

73. Hawkins, "The Coming of the Russian Ships in 1863.

74. Morison, Samuel Eliot, *John Paul Jones: A Sailor's Biography* (Boston: Little, Brown and Co., 1959).

75. Proceedings of the American Philosophical Society, 91:1947.

76. Boynton, Rev. Charles B., *The Four Great Powers: England, France, Russia and America; Their Policy. Resources, and Probable Future* (Cincinnati, Chicago: C.F. Vent and Co., 1866).

77. *Ibid.*

78. *Diary of Gideon Welles* (3 vols., 1911), Vol. 1, p. 443.

79. *Harper's Weekly*, Oct. 17, 1863.

80. *Ibid.*

81. *Ibid.*

82. *Harper's New Monthly Magazine*, Vol. 27 (1863), p. 848.

83. *Harper's Weekly*, Oct. 17, 1863.

84. Balch, *The Alabama Arbitration*. pp. 28-31.

85. *Ibid.*

86. Adams, *Great Britain and the American Civil War*, Vol. 2.

87. Lincoln, Abraham, *Complete Works of Abraham Lincoln*, edited by John G. Nicolay and John Hay (New York: Lamb Publishing Co., 1905), Vol. 6.

88. W. Read West, "Contemporary French Opinion on the American Civil War," *Johns Hopkins University Studies in History and Political Science*, 1924. Quotation is from *La Patrie* of January 12, 1864.

89. Robertson, James R., *A Kentuckian at the Court of the Tsars* (Berea, Kentucky: Berea College Press, 1935).

90. *Ibid.*

91. *Harper's Weekly*, Oct. 17, 1863.

92. Robertson, *A Kentuckian at the Court of the Tsars*.

93. *Ibid.*

94. Loubat, J.F., *Fox's Mission to Russia*.

95. *Ibid.*

96. *Ibid.*

97. *Ibid.*

98. *Ibid.*

99. *New York Herald.* April 29, 1876.

Made in the USA
Middletown, DE
08 November 2020